Why Are You So Sensitive?

NAVIGATING EVERYDAY, UNINTENDED MICROAGGRESSIONS

BILLIE LEE

WITH DR. GINA C. TORINO

Andrews McMeel
PUBLISHING®

Andrews McMeel Publishing
a division of Andrews McMeel Universal
1130 Walnut Street, Kansas City, Missouri 64106

www.andrewsmcmeel.com

24 25 26 27 IGO 10 9 8 7 6 5 4 3 2 1

ISBN: 978-1-5248-7349-3

Library of Congress Control Number: 2023948109

Editors: Marya Pasciuto, Betty Wong
Art Director: Diane Marsh
Production Editor: Jasmine Lim
Production Manager: Chadd Keim

Illustrations by Jackie Rivera

ATTENTION: SCHOOLS AND BUSINESSES
Andrews McMeel books are available at quantity discounts with bulk purchase for educational, business, or sales promotional use. For information, please e-mail the Andrews McMeel Publishing Special Sales Department: sales@amuniversal.com.

*I dedicate this book to my trans and nonbinary
community, with whom I found true self-love
and acceptance; to all those who've dealt with
discrimination for just being who they are;
and to my friends, family, and mentors who've
loved and accepted me unconditionally.*

CONTENTS

CHAPTER 1:
FRIENDS AND FAMILY
1

CHAPTER 2:
DATING AND RELATIONSHIPS
27

CHAPTER 3:
WORKPLACE
57

CHAPTER 4:
STRANGERS AND ACQUAINTANCES
91

Introduction

A couple of years ago, I was at a climate rally where I ran into a model friend of mine. The girl is drop-dead gorgeous and a very vocal mental health advocate, speaking often about her experience being bipolar. As we stood there with our signs, surrounded by people and sweaty from protesting, she took a moment to marvel at the contradictions she embodied: how she loves fashion and beauty products but also loves the planet and would happily get dirty in the fight to protect it. I jumped in, saying, "I know, girl! Me, too! It's like we're both bipolar trying to save the planet." As soon as the words left my mouth, I wanted to kick myself—how could I have said that?! Her face fell, and she gave me a look that said, "Really? Did my trans activist friend just use being bipolar as a joke?" I felt so bad. I gave her an awkward goodbye and crept away with my "How dare you" sign.

My intentions had been pure—I wanted to bond with my friend about these shared passions and parts of our identities—but my intentions weren't what mattered. I had made a major mistake. In using "bipolar" as a joke, I'd minimized her experience living with an incredibly challenging disorder. I forgot about the power words have to hurt someone, to make them feel uncomfortable and less than. I was wrong, and I later apologized to her, but in my head, I continued to beat myself up: I felt like I should have known better. I myself had been the victim of so many macro- and microaggressions in my life, and I considered myself educated and sensitive, so shouldn't I have realized what I was doing?

Microaggressions are defined as brief and commonplace verbal, behavioral, or environmental indignities, whether intentional or unintentional, that communicate hostile, derogatory, or negative prejudicial slights and insults toward any group—particularly culturally marginalized groups.

Some of the earliest microaggressions I remember experiencing came from my father: I was a fragile, sensitive, and feminine child, which seemed to bother him to no end. He was always yelling at me to "Be a man!" "Put those muscles into it!" "Don't be a sissy, boy!" "Get strong and buff up like your brother!" The more he used those phrases, the more ashamed I felt. Something about me was different and wrong: I was too weak, too girly, and not the man my dad wanted me to be.

I know he never meant to hurt me. (Later, when I was transitioning, my dad would actually become my lifeline when he called me out of the blue to say, "Billie, I want you to know if you decide to wear a dress and be a woman, I'll walk you down the aisle at your wedding." It was exactly the support I needed and one of the kindest things anyone has ever done for me.) My dad loved me, and at the time, he might have even thought that he was helping me by encouraging me to be the best version of what I was "supposed" to be—a tough and strong little boy. But that's the danger of microaggressions—they are often disguised as something totally innocent: an act of love, a common expression, a joke. It's why, even for those of us who consider ourselves incredibly socially conscious, we can still be guilty of expressing a microaggression and causing harm.

MICROAGGRESSIONS ARE
COMMONPLACE VERBAL, BEHAVIORAL,
OR ENVIRONMENTAL INDIGNITIES,
WHETHER INTENTIONAL OR
UNINTENTIONAL, THAT COMMUNICATE
NEGATIVE PREJUDICIAL SLIGHTS.

If we're lucky, we can catch ourselves before the words escape our lips or, if we're too late, apologize and hopefully be forgiven. But sometimes, we might not be aware that what we're saying is harmful—especially if our intentions are noble ones. After I transitioned, I was flooded with compliments like, "Oh, Billie, you look just like a real girl! I couldn't even tell" and "Wow, Billie, you look so much more like a girl than any other trans girl I've met" and even "Wow, you are so sexy I would f*ck you, and I don't f*ck dudes, so that's a compliment."

See, the people "complimenting" me didn't think they were doing anything wrong; they didn't realize the microaggressions were not only hurting me but hurting my community. Imagine all these trans women behind me— some are taller, some are wider, and some present more masculine than I appear. Some can't afford all the surgeries I received. Does that not make them beautiful? My community is a part of me. When I hear these types of microaggressions disguised as compliments, it makes me sad. If we don't all fit in this very feminine box, are we not worthy of your love and acceptance?

These thoughts have been swirling inside my mind for a long time. Every time I heard a microaggression uttered in public or caught myself about to use one, my frustration would bubble up inside me.

SOMETIMES, WE MIGHT NOT BE AWARE THAT WHAT WE'RE SAYING IS HARMFUL.

Why don't more people know how harmful these comments can be, how deeply they can cut? One day, it hit me: with all the privileges I had—a large public platform and the support of so many activists and celebrities whom I considered friends—maybe I could actually do something about it! I had the means to share my knowledge about microaggressions with others and have my voice heard. And where my knowledge and lived experience ended, I could find others to share their own truths and lived experiences. I wanted to gather all this information into what could hopefully become an intersectional resource free of judgment—an educational tool that would not only inspire readers to do better for themselves and those around them but affirm the experience of those who have suffered from such harm.

The result is this book, which you are now holding in your hands.

Making this book taught me so much. The contributors you'll hear from on these pages come from a range of intersectional backgrounds and upbringings, and speaking with them taught me how important it is to recognize those differences when we communicate with one another. I was shocked to find, for example, that people whom I viewed as privileged, whom I wouldn't have expected to experience harm in ways similar to myself, also endured daily microaggressions. There were also so many moments in which I related so deeply to my contributors; despite our clear differences, we shared a keen desire to feel loved and included and validated for our own unique lived experiences. I hope that you, too, feel seen and heard as you read this book. We are not all alike, and our differences are what make us so amazing.

I'm so thankful to all of my contributors. It's never easy to rehash a painful experience, so I am in deep gratitude for your willingness to share your stories here.

I often think of the old saying, "When you know better, you do better." The fact that you picked up this book means that you're curious about and/or committed to effecting positive change through your words and are trying to understand more deeply the lived experiences of people different from yourself. I applaud you! But—and this is a big "but"!—please know that this book is by no means exhaustive. While I have tried to include individuals representing a wide range of identities, there is no way that I could fit everyone's lived experience and every microaggression into this book. So what does that mean for you and me? It means that this is just the beginning—read this book and learn. Then go and read more books. Educate yourself and others. Catch yourself before you let a microaggression slip out. If you do say it, know that it's okay—apologize and commit to doing better in the future. If it's safe to do so, help others understand the harm of microaggressions that they may be using in their conversations with you.

Ultimately, I hope that this book will prevent another person from feeling small—like how I've been made to feel in my life and how I made my friend feel at the rally that day—and thus shield larger communities from harm. I'm not perfect, I'm not the most educated person, and I still have to learn some things the hard way. We are human, and we are capable of error, and writing this book does not make me perfect. But I hope it helps us all do better. I want it to be a tool for us to use in everyday life—to jump-start our awareness about microaggressions so that we can all help make the world a kinder, more beautiful place to live in.

—BILLIE LEE

UNDERSTANDING MICROAGGRESSIONS

Dr. Gina C. Torino

"*Y*ou're so articulate." "You speak good English." "There is only one race, the human race." These are only a few examples of the subtle form of discrimination called microaggressions. Microaggressions occur daily and can appear in speech, writing, behavior, and even the surrounding environment. They are rooted in stereotypes we hold about others and are often done unintentionally due to our unconscious biases.

The term "microaggression" was introduced in the 1970s in the groundbreaking work of Dr. Chester Pierce, a renowned Harvard psychiatrist. Dr. Daniel Solórzano further delved into the experience of microaggressions among students of color in college. I was fortunate enough to be on the research team, led by Dr. Derald Wing Sue, that published one of the most influential articles on the topic: "Racial Microaggressions in Everyday Life." The article provides a comprehensive framework for understanding microaggressions and has contributed significantly to the public understanding and discussion of this phenomenon. After the article's publication in 2007, a wide range of studies was undertaken to explore the impact of microaggressions throughout our society. The term entered the mainstream, and in 2017 the term "microaggression" was officially added to the pages of *Merriam-Webster's* dictionary. This concept has also been portrayed in such television shows as *Black-ish, Unbreakable Kimmy Schmidt*, and others.

So why are microaggressions so important? Some have argued that microaggressions are harmless slights and that focusing on microaggressions fosters a culture of victimhood, suppresses free speech, and "coddles" people. However, microaggressions can in fact cause harm *because* of their subtlety, which makes them difficult to identify as intentional and so problematic to confront and resolve. Moreover, research shows that experiencing microaggressions day after day, year after year, can have an insidious effect and can be a sort of "death by a thousand cuts." Studies have shown that experiencing numerous microaggressions over time has a cumulative impact that can be extremely harmful to the recipient, or "target," of the microaggressions. The experience of microaggressions has been connected to employment problems, cognitive issues, anxiety, depression, traumatic stress, suicidal thoughts, and impaired physical health.

You may be thinking, "This is interesting, but I don't commit microaggressions." Well, unfortunately, none of us are immune to having biases against members of other groups. We may not be aware of our biases, but we do have them. Throughout my childhood and early adulthood as a White, heterosexual, lower-middle-class, Catholic, cisgender woman of Italian American ancestry, I was unaware that I held any biases at all. After all, I had African American friends and family members. My ex was biracial. I had gay friends. Growing up, my best friend was Filipino. So how could *I* be biased? When I was in graduate school training to be a psychologist, I participated in a course called the Racial Cultural Counseling Laboratory. In this course, I looked at my own group memberships, such as race, ethnicity, social class, and religion, and how they shaped my thoughts and feelings about myself and people from other groups. I was asked to confront my preconceived notions about others. This was a demanding task filled with uncomfortable emotions such as fear, shame, and guilt. My experience in the "lab" transformed not only my career but my life: it was in this course that I first learned the immense importance of coming to grips with one's unconscious or implicit biases. I began to realize the harm that these implicit biases can cause for individuals and the larger society when they are expressed as microaggressions.

WE ALL COMMIT MICROAGGRESSIONS; THE KEY IS TO KEEP WORKING AT BEING BETTER.

In this important collection of poignant and timely personal narratives, Billie Lee has assembled many real-life examples of microaggressions that have been experienced by people of many different backgrounds and shed light on the widespread effects of microaggressions. The personal narratives illustrate the experiences of numerous marginalized communities, encompassing those defined by race, ethnicity, gender, LGBTQ+ identity, ability, body size, mental illness, intersectional identities, and beyond. Here, you will find both unique and familiar accounts of microaggressions from various sources, including family members, friends, coworkers, strangers, and romantic or sexual partners. Through these compelling narratives, you will gain a better understanding of how seemingly benign acts can have long-lasting impacts.

Throughout the book, I offer guidance and tactics on how to respond to microaggressions if you encounter them, how to stop yourself from committing microaggressions, and how to respond if someone confronts you when you slip up. I say *when*, not *if*, because we all commit microaggressions; the key is to keep working at being better. To that end, at the back of the book, I provide resources to assist you in investigating the topic as well as places where you can find support for your experience.

Confronting microaggressions is a lifelong journey, and the best way to do it is to understand other people's perspectives. As the narratives in this book prompt you to reflect on your own emotions and experiences, you will learn not only how microaggressions affect the lives of others but also how they play a role in your own life.

ON
MICROAGGRESSIONS

Jane Velez-Mitchell

*M*icroaggressions. The thing about them is that they make you doubt yourself. Did that really happen, or am I imagining it? Was she being hostile, or am I just overly sensitive? Am I right to feel hurt or . . . am I crazy?

If you felt it, it happened.

Microaggressions are the subtle attacks that leave no visible marks, but the invisible cuts still sting.

"If you felt it,

IT HAPPENED."

—Jane Velez-Mitchell

CHAPTER 1

Friends and Family

"Are you sure
THIS IS THE RIGHT
choice for you?"

*W*hen I announced I was starting hormones and would be getting sexual reassignment surgery, everyone questioned whether I was making the right choice: my friends, coworkers, and family. It seemed like everyone had an opinion and they just *had* to pipe up to let me know it. I realize it came from a place of love, but it was so incredibly frustrating and even damaging to suggest that I didn't know what I wanted or that what I wanted was wrong. Making someone feel wrong about something so major and personal is detrimental to one's personality and identity.

I knew this was the right choice for me because I knew it would finally mean freedom: I would get to be *me* and fully free to express my femininity without constantly being made to feel ashamed of it. But it was also difficult and scary to medically transition with hormones and major surgeries and to hear people constantly express doubt about a choice that felt so right. That just made it harder because any transition in life can be isolating. There is so much unknown, and feeling supported makes all the difference.

Years later, the questions and comments began again. And it's even worse now because as we get older, we become wiser and more secure in our life decisions. I've started the adoption process to adopt a child, and people are constantly questioning this choice that I know in my heart to be true. I am so excited and sure that becoming a mommy—finally—is the right decision for me. But I also know with adoption, it's not just about me. There's another human life involved, and of course, I feel doubt about becoming a single parent—it will be hard! These questions ping-pong around constantly in my head. Can I handle it? Will I do a good job? Will I be enough? But guess what: these are questions that all expecting parents ask themselves. When an outside party, whether it's a loved one or an acquaintance, asks, "Are you sure this is the right choice?" what they're *really* saying is that they have doubts about your judgment and capabilities, and they think you should reconsider whatever choice you're about to make.

Instead of questioning my decisions, what I really need from you is support. Because in asking me, *"Aren't you afraid of making a big mistake? What if it's not the right time? Are you sure this is what you want? What if you have regrets? You can't go back, so make sure this is what you really want . . .,"* you're not bringing up anything I haven't already thought through myself. And what you might be intending as an expression of love instead makes me feel like I don't know what I'm doing. That's the last thing I need when I'm about to make an informed, thought-out decision.

Instead of telling me that the outcome of my choice will be hard and scary and I shouldn't undertake such a journey, tell me it's going to be hard and scary—and that you'll be there for me.

EXPERT TAKE: As Billie mentions, questions from close family members often come from a place of real concern about the major decisions in the lives of their loved ones. However, the approach her family and friends took did more harm than good. If a loved one comes to you with an update like Billie's, it's best to recognize how much thought went into their choice, trust that they're doing what's right for them, and express support in a way that respects their autonomy. Instead of questioning their decision, try offering more helpful questions like, "Is there anything I can do to help you during your transition?" or "How can I support you through this process?"

"YOU'RE NOT REALLY BLACK"

Christine Ahanotu

I remember the first time someone told me I wasn't "really" Black. They meant it as a compliment. To imply that I was lucky. That I could technically escape the tropes of American Blackness because my mother was Irish and I had grown up with a Eurocentric understanding of the world. That I had "good" hair (not a thing). That I spoke "proper" English.

Regardless of the fact that my father was Nigerian, born in Enugu State, one of ten children who moved to America and all found varying degrees of success.

Regardless of the fact that my skin was the color of coffee with light cream, getting deeper under the summer sun.

Love me . . . or hate me. But I am me.

Your opinion is not needed.

Regardless of the fact . . .

I wasn't "really" Black . . . so racism didn't apply to me.

I was one of them.

I have had family members say it.

Strangers.

Lovers. (Those are the worst.)

And the thing is, I didn't disagree with them. I wasn't really . . . or rather, "solely" Black. I am a child of two parents from opposite ends of the planet who somehow managed to meet, fall in love, and have me.

I am a girl who grew up on Igbo music and Chopin. I have definitely spent more time around my white family members than my Black ones.

But I am also, most definitely, Black.

Not just because that is how the world views me.

But because I AM.

I am also white.

Go figure.

So the next time you approach your biracial friend or family member with good intentions and before you tell them what they "really" are, just remember: they are all of those things . . . and more. And your opinion on their Blackness or whiteness or gayness or straightness or weirdness or squareness or what the f*** ever . . . your opinion is not the point.

Love me . . . or hate me. But I AM me.

Your opinion is not needed.

EXPERT TAKE: Here, it is important to note the difference between intention and impact. If you find yourself with the desire to "compliment" a biracial friend or family member by telling them they are not "really" Black, it may be good to check your thought before you speak and recognize it may be coming from negative stereotypes about Black people.

"YOU'RE NOT 'LIKE THEM'"

Jazzmyne Jay

*G*rowing up in a predominantly white area with a Black father and a white mother, whenever friends or strangers made a racist statement about Black people in front of me, they would follow it up by saying of course they weren't talking about me and my family because we weren't "like them." I didn't know what to say back—I was somewhere between hurt and afraid to confront them on their racism. I wish I had the voice I have now.

Expert Take: It is crucial to understand one's own biases when it comes to race. So, the perpetrator in this case may question, "What does 'them' mean?" By doing this, one can increase self-awareness and identify prejudices or misconceptions about Black people. This could go a long way to prevent microaggressions.

"SHE DOESN'T EVEN LOOK INDIGENOUS"

ANONYMOUS

I just got home when my phone rang. It was my partner. I was excited to see his name light up my phone, but my face soon dropped as he voiced to me that he was upset with his grandparents. While they were in the kitchen together, he overheard them saying, "¡Qué bonita! She's so pretty; she doesn't even look like an 'indio.'" My partner defensively asked for clarification and proceeded to tell them that I was, in fact, Indigenous and that they, too, are Indigenous people of Nicaragua. In denial, they started yelling back and forth and eventually departed to their own rooms.

My heart started racing, and my face burned. There was so much to unpack and process in the conversation. I'm grateful I wasn't there in person because I'm sure I would've cried. Soon childhood memories of anxiously scrubbing the "dirt" from my skin in a boiling bathtub flooded my mind. The smell of sunscreen filling my nose as my grandparents tried to keep me from basking in the sunlight so I wouldn't get darker. Remembering all the times my grandmother told me to brush my "long, scraggly Apache hair."

I felt invalidated. I was only a child when I learned that having "European features" made me beautiful, and because of those beauty standards, I still struggle with my own self-image. I had scrubbed and starved and buried the person I am because I wanted to be beautiful when deep down, I wanted to feel valued. I had to learn to love my features: cheekbones high enough that when my mom and I laughed too hard on a phone call, we would accidentally hang up, moles on my face that make me look like a tortilla according to my partner, small eyes that turn into rainbows when I smile. However, that comment seemed to leave a lump in my throat and remind me of the long nights scrubbing in the shower.

But I was not the only collateral in this conversation. My partner also voiced to me how heavy that comment made them feel. He, too, had shared his memory of scrubbing at his skin as a child because he was too dark, or how he always had to be conscious of his appearance out of fear of being mistaken for another person by police, or how he was never validated by his family because of the way he looks.

I think the saddest part of it all was that his grandparents could not recognize that they had hurt themselves. They are Indigenous, just like my partner and me and yet still believe that having more "European features" makes someone more beautiful.

I hope that to the individual reading this, that you, too, recognize the beauty in yourself for not just who you are and the journey you've made but also the temple that nurtured you along the way. And to my body, I am sorry for being so cruel to you for simply existing.

EXPERT TAKE: Over time, experiencing microaggressions like these can take a toll on one's self-worth. Finding supportive allies and community members in person or online who can understand and validate your experience is really important. That support and pride in your culture can help create an emotional buffer in moments like those this person experienced and help protect you from the harmful impact of negative stereotypes.

"I DON'T KNOW HOW YOU GET UP WITH A SMILE EVERY DAY"

JOCELYN MONDRAGON-ROSAS

I was about to take the first sip of my early-morning coffee when my caregiver said, "I don't know how you get up with a smile every day." I wanted to say it was due to the coffee. Instead, I didn't say anything and took my first sip to prepare me for the rest of the ableist things she was about to say.

It's true that when you have a disability, you do struggle. Sometimes you find smiling is easier than talking about when you're having a high chronic pain day. Sometimes putting on a smile or even making a joke is easier than showing frustration at your local coffee shop for taking away straws. Sometimes putting on a smile and moving on with your day is easier than being in a constant fight for access and respect from the world.

When nondisabled people say things like, "I don't know how you get up with a smile every day," it makes me question what they think of my existence. Do they think I'm always sad? Do they think I see my life as a burden? Do they think I force myself to live each day? Yes, I struggle sometimes. I don't know anyone, even people without disabilities, who hasn't ever struggled, and yet I don't question anyone's existence or how they get up in the morning.

There's this common yet unspoken assumption from nondisabled people that either you have to be super positive about your life with a disability and its struggles or you hate your life so much you force yourself to get up every day. This assumption doesn't leave room for disabled people to be content with where we're at. This assumption also reduces our feelings and experiences to being only black and white when we know humans and our emotions are much more complex than that.

Yes, living with a disability or illness can be hard, but it's not fair to reduce our lives to just pain. It's kind of like when a person with a disability dies and someone says, "They're no longer in pain" or "Now they're free." Again, we might have experienced pain from our disabilities or illnesses, but that's not all that we experience. We have love and joy in our lives, and we also have anger and sadness in our lives—and believe it or not, it doesn't always have to do with our disability. I mean, the other day I was just upset that I couldn't get a Caramel Frappé from McDonald's because the machine was broken.

I understand some people may need hope to get by every day, but please don't make us into your inspiration just for living our lives with disabilities. Please don't question my existence. Our disabled existence isn't here to make you feel better about your nondisabled existence.

EXPERT TAKE: It is critical to remember that just because someone has different abilities does not imply that they are inferior or that their life is less fulfilling or joyful. If you find yourself thinking the way the perpetrator of this microaggression did, take a moment to consider that varied abilities can be strengths. Rather than sharing this potentially harmful opinion with a disabled person, it's best to examine your own thoughts for a moment to see if you really need to communicate them.

FATPHOBIC "JOKES"

ALEXANDRA FOLSTER

"Who's that on the ground, a beached whale?" I remember hearing my grandfather say after Christmas dinner. My body image and weight were always "too much" for others.

I never understood why they couldn't just love me for me, when all I've wanted was to love myself.

EXPERT TAKE: Some people still think it's acceptable to mock people with large bodies. It's really important to remember that calling a family member, especially a young child, names like "beached whale" can cause pain that stays with them for years to come. No joke is worth the negativity that Alexandra's grandfather inflicted with his comment—remember this if you ever feel like making a similar comment, especially when speaking to a loved one.

"YOU'RE NOT A REAL PERSON OF COLOR"

STEPHANIE KWONG

I once left an event with a friend who said, "I'm surprised there weren't any people of color at that party." I said, "But I was there. I'm a person of color," to which she replied, "Yeah, but you don't count. I'm talking about a real person of color—you blend in." We went back and forth on it for a while, and I couldn't believe I had to convince her of my own identity. She finally acknowledged I was a person of color, but only because Wikipedia confirmed it; it was dismissive, frustrating, and hurtful and left me feeling completely unheard. My experiences, identity, and truth weren't enough to deem me an authority figure on my own self.

EXPERT TAKE: If a loved one pushes back against something you say about their identity, it is important to take them at their word. When a friend implies or directly states that you have perpetrated a microaggression, it's best to apologize right away instead of doubling down like what happened in this situation. It's natural to feel defensive in moments like this but try to recognize in the moment that your loved one has taken a risk by being vulnerable enough to question your comment; apologizing, rather than responding defensively, will help maintain your friendship and strengthen trust between you.

"ALL MICROAGGRESSIONS *are rooted in fear.* FEAR OF THE *unknown.* FEAR OF *rejection,* FEAR OF *failure,* FEAR OF ONE'S OWN *reflection* IN OTHERS."

—CAROLINA GUTIERREZ

PRESSURE TO PEE

Jeremiah Ripley

After years of failed surgeries to "fix" my intersex variation, I have been left with scarring tissue. This means it usually takes me longer to use the restroom, a fact that has embarrassed me since I was a child. That embarrassment has been made worse by the barrage of comments I receive, sometimes while I'm even still using the restroom. Comments like:

"Are you almost done in there?"

"What are you doing in there?"

"Did everything come out okay?"

"Did you fall in?"

"You were in there forever."

EXPERT TAKE: People on the receiving end of comments like this one are in a difficult position since it may be difficult to express one's innermost feelings about private matters to others who do not share one's experience. If this happens to you, try deflecting or disarming the microaggressions with a more neutral, even playful-seeming response like, "What an odd thing to say!" Such a response gently calls attention to the fact that these comments are out of line, and it might provide an opportunity for the microaggressor to reflect on their own.

"Stop being so loud."

I'm from a very big and loud family—when we're together, we're a swirling mass of jokes, laughter, yelling, and swearing. It's admittedly a lot! As a quiet, and at times, introverted individual, I have had to learn to navigate this loving chaos with patience and care. Occasionally, when I need a break, I'll slip away for a bit of peace by taking a walk barefoot or going to visit the animals at nearby farms. With that said, I wouldn't change my family for the world.

Some of my family's loudness has sprung from necessity. My grandmother experienced significant hearing loss from domestic violence when she was a young adult, and she struggled to hear the world around her. So, naturally, my mother and her thirteen—yes, thirteen!—siblings learned to speak loudly to accommodate my grandmother. It was the natural way in which they communicated with one another, and it was never a problem unless they had to ask their sister four seats down to pass the popcorn at the movie theater. Ha!

Even after my mother moved out of her family's house and moved in with my dad at the age of fifteen, she didn't turn the volume dial down on her speech. And why would she? Her loud laugh was infectious, and hearing her tell a sly joke with a smile in her voice made everyone around her happier.

I don't know the exact moment when my father met my mother— maybe he heard her before he saw her?! Regardless of how they met, they quickly fell in love and got married at sixteen while my mother was still pregnant with me.

But from the time I was a young child, I can remember my father cutting his eyes at my mom, hissing at her to "Keep it down!" or "Stop being so loud!" especially when we were in public. I'm sure he didn't consciously realize this in these moments, but whenever he directed my mother to be quiet, what he was really doing was asking her to make herself smaller, to fold herself up and take up less space in the world.

Over the years, my mother shrank into herself. I'd notice that she would correct herself by lowering her voice or covering her mouth after bursting out with a particularly big laugh. Her infectious personality became muted after the innumerable times that my father told her to be quiet.

What ended up happening? My mother couldn't make herself any smaller. Her natural joy had left her. There were only so many times my father could reject my mother after she showed him who she really was before the relationship shattered. They ended up divorcing after twenty years of marriage. Sometimes I wondered if my father felt the silence he had created by driving my mother away was louder than when they were together.

Of course, this simplifies things a bit—my parents had other problems that they dealt with, other disagreements that forced them apart. But as a close observer of their relationship, I learned a valuable lesson. Don't try to silence someone you love. When you do so, you are asking them to change their authentic self to fit into a box of your making. Take them as they are—big belly laugh and all.

EXPERT TAKE: It is essential that we acknowledge the possibility that our partners and family members have a variety of ways of expressing themselves. It can be hard to push back when on the receiving end of comments like Billie's father made, so if it happens to you, put your own comfort first. If confronting the issue directly doesn't feel best for you in the moment, try to remind yourself that you have the absolute right to express yourself and that others around you love your vivacious nature and contagious laughter.

"YOU MUST BE GOOD AT . . ."

REBECCA BARNES

*B*eing a Jewish woman, I've heard almost every microaggression, but the ones that bother me most are "You must be good at making matzah balls since you're Jewish" and "You must be good at saving money because all Jews are rich."

Just because someone is Jewish does not make them rich, nor does it make them chefs when it comes to matzah balls. Not all Jewish people express their religion the same.

Just like all humans are not the same, all Jewish people are also not the same.

EXPERT TAKE: Many people have preconceived notions about Jewish people based on cultural and religious stereotypes—even if they hold them subconsciously. Comments like the ones expressed here are experienced as "othering" even though they are meant as praise. Context here is important! It's totally fine to compliment a loved one on their cooking, but you can do it without making their identity group so central. (And if you're not being served a traditional dish or being offered financial advice by a Jewish friend, there's no reason to invoke stereotypes related to those things.)

ASSUMING I'LL BE UNCOMFORTABLE

JENNIFER P.

Growing up, I never identified as Filipino. I don't think I really understood what an ethnic background or race was until high school. It probably didn't matter much to me until it was obvious that image was important. That status was important. What everyone thought about you was important—which for most, like myself, made high school important.

I distinctly remember this one time when some girls from our basketball team were going to go out dancing. We were texting back and forth about the plan. I was really excited. One of my teammates who was one of those popular, wealthy white girls called me up. She let me know who would be going out with us. I didn't really hang out with any of these kids, but I thought it would be a good opportunity to get to know them better. So when I said, "Okay, where should we meet?" She said something like, "I think you are going to be uncomfortable if you go since . . . [she went on to name friends of mine who were all minorities] won't be there." Everyone going was white, wealthy, and family friends. "It's probably best if you don't come."

I just didn't see a point in confronting her. Her words felt like little jabs under my ribs. I kept my head down. The divide was real.

The problem was I would never be white, and I didn't know what it meant to be Filipino. And so image was important. Status was important. Skin color was important.

EXPERT TAKE: Assuming how comfortable your friend would be in a multiracial group event is just that: an assumption. Jennifer's teammate may have thought she was being helpful, but she should have taken Jennifer at her word when she expressed excitement about the event and asked logistical questions about meeting up—by assuming Jennifer would be uncomfortable among wealthy white people, she put her assumptions about Jennifer's identity before Jennifer's own words. In situations like this, it's best to take your friend at their word—feel free to check in if they express discomfort, but don't jump to conclusions about another's wishes based on their identity alone.

"YOU CAN FINISH THAT"

KO WILLS

*O*ver the years while dining with friends and family, I've experienced many microaggressions at the table. The most common assumption is that someone like me can finish not only my plate but theirs as well. Assuming a plus-size person eats more than they should. Not all plus-size people overeat; some have thyroid and other medical issues that have nothing to do with food.

Never assume the size of my body determines how much I eat, because plus-size people are healthy and make healthy choices.

EXPERT TAKE: If you receive a comment like this from a loved one and feel comfortable with a direct response, try calling attention to the underlying meaning of the microaggression: "Are you saying that because of the size of my body, I can eat both my food and yours?" Laying bare the meaning behind their words like this provides the individual who did it a chance to reflect on what they said.

"ACT LIKE A MAN"

MITCHELL FAHEY

Since I was young, I've been a very sensitive person, closely in touch with my emotional side. My mom said it was a blessing, not a curse, but I didn't always see it from that perspective because I did not fit in with other men's versions of how I should be in this world. I'd often receive unsolicited advice in the form of societal expectations or simply nasty verbal microaggressions from peers about how I should be acting to be a "man" and what emotions I was allowed to or not allowed to express.

As I got older and learned more about myself, I realized the internal homophobia I had developed from these experiences and learned to heal and grow with the help of therapy, community, and plenty of self-actualization. I've realized that we don't have to be or become what others expect us to be; that choice is up to us.

EXPERT TAKE: It is essential for people who face homophobic microaggressions to put their own comfort and safety first. In the moment, it's okay not to push back against people who treat you with cruelty like Mitchell's peers did; try to remind yourself that your expression is valid and that there's no "right" way to be a man. More broadly, putting yourself first may mean connecting with supportive communities online or in person or seeking emotional support from trusted friends, allies, or professionals. Surrounding yourself with positive and affirming messages and people can help counteract the cumulative impact of experiencing anti-LGBTQ microaggressions.

CONCLUSION:

IT CAN be challenging when people whom we deeply value in our lives, such as family members and close friends, convey negative comments to us—and it can be hard to reckon with the harm we unintentionally commit against our loved ones, too. The interpersonal dynamics within close familial and friend relationships, however, present a unique opportunity to work on reducing harm. Given the recurring nature of these interactions, individuals who perpetrate microaggressions can build on our existing bonds with our loved ones and build a better understanding of our actions.

For example, it is crucial to practice providing authentic compliments based on individual attributes rather than focusing on their identity groups (e.g., race, gender, sexual orientation) and to take people at their word instead of questioning their judgment or becoming defensive when called out. This behavior can extend to our interactions with individuals whom we are less familiar with, such as new partners, colleagues, strangers, and acquaintances. Seeking out learning opportunities (such as those listed at the conclusion of this book) can help you develop greater self-awareness, allowing you to respond to and possibly prevent microaggressions involving friends and family members in your own life.

For the recipients of microaggressions, family and friendships may be an easier environment for learning and practicing the skills of responding to microaggressions presented in this chapter, such as disarming a comment or prioritizing one's own comfort in the wake of an uncomfortable moment. In these longer-term relationships, you may be more comfortable opening a dialogue in a quiet moment—the goal is always to take care of ourselves and those around us, with the hope that the friends and family who care about us will meet us halfway.

CHAPTER 2

Dating and Relationships

"I WAS JUST joking"

BILLIE LEE

*I*t started at an early age. Most of the time when I'd hear the phrase "I was just joking," it came from school bullies after they'd said something hurtful to me, like "Billie, you have a girl's voice" or "Billie's a sissy." But the time that hurt me the most was during my first relationship at sixteen. The guy I was secretly dating was a few years older than me, smart, and handsome, but he loved picking apart my femininity as if it were on a shelf for display. "Billie, why are you wearing makeup?" He didn't want me to shave my legs and always encouraged me to wear more masculine clothing. "Billie, you're a boy; I'm dating a boy; act like one." He always brushed aside his harsh comments with a glib "I was just joking." It was as if he thought that one phrase would erase the hurt I felt. It didn't.

As an adult, I expected I would finally have the language to push back against such behavior, but I found that it simply was not that easy. A few years back, a former partner brandished the phrase at mealtimes. See, I've always been a fast eater. As a child, it was a survival mechanism because the longer I stayed at the dinner table, the more my family picked my femininity apart. My brother would tell my parents all the rumors about me at school: "Dad, Billie shaves his legs" or "Mom, did you know your son sucks dick?" My brother's rumor report always ended with me in tears, so I quickly learned the faster I ate all my food, the faster I could go back to my room.

Eventually eating fast became the norm, and it brought me comfort. But as an adult, it morphed into binge eating, an unhealthy habit that brought me a lot of shame. Still, to this day, when I feel ashamed, I turn to binge eating. My favorite is taking an entire package of Oreos, dumping them into a large bowl with ice-cold almond milk, and eating the entire bowl with a fork. Or secretly ordering a cheese pizza, devouring the entire pie in minutes, and then washing it down with a large soda.

The worst was while out to dinner, my previous partner would comment on how fast I finished my food. At first, I would fake laugh it off, but it always hit a nerve. I even started counting while I ate to help me eat slower. I eventually explained to my partner where the habit came from and how awful their comments made me feel. But they didn't listen, continuing to call me out in different ways: "Damn, babe. You tore that up" or "Wow, babe, you were hungry." And then there it was, the "I was just joking" to dismiss my feelings.

WHAT'S DANGEROUS ABOUT "I WAS JUST JOKING" IS THAT IT LETS PEOPLE THINK THEY'RE OFF THE HOOK.

But microaggressions are tricky, and being the victim of a microaggression doesn't mean we can never also be the antagonist perpetrating harm. While dating a much younger guy from my acting class, I quickly became annoyed by his immature behavior. I would comment, "Can you please grow up?" or "Please act your age." But often then feel a wave of guilt wash over me so I would immediately follow with "I was just joking" to smooth things over. It wasn't fair for me to judge this young adult, who still had so much growing up to do, let alone dismiss my negative comments with the same microaggression that had been used against me. When I eventually ended the relationship, I spoke openly about my feelings and apologized to him. He would brush it off and quickly change the subject, but I know it didn't make him feel good. I'm thankful we grew our relationship into a solid friendship.

Ultimately, what's so dangerous about "I was just joking" is that it lets people think they're off the hook for their poor behavior. It makes it easy for them to claim they have no responsibility and shouldn't face any

DATING AND RELATIONSHIPS

consequences for their "joking" behavior. It is used as a distraction to dismiss and minimize the pain they have caused.

Let's not hide behind harmful microaggressions like "I'm just joking" because acknowledging it could make all the difference in someone's life.

EXPERT TAKE: Someone who commits a microaggression might say they were joking, but that doesn't make it okay. The comment may be delivered in a humorous way, but the literal meaning of the speaker's words stays the same, expressing an implicit bias that can be damaging. If someone says that you have delivered a microaggression and you find yourself wanting to respond with "I was just joking," pause and reflect on what you just said or did and then offer an apology. Even if you did mean it as a joke, your loved one has decided to be vulnerable in telling you that it wasn't funny to them. This understanding can go a long way. Use the experience as an opportunity to seek out possibilities for growth; some useful resources are available at the end of this book.

31

"I USED TO BE BISEXUAL"

ZACHARY ZANE

*T*his is a response I've heard from countless gay men when I share that I'm romantically and sexually attracted to all genders. While I'm not out here flaunting my bisexuality—all right, I am a little bit—I do like to correct people when they falsely assume that I am gay. Given my limp wrists, affinity for crop tops, and high-pitched "Yas kween," that's quite often.

At first, their response didn't bother me. I figured these gay men, many of whom are a decade or two older than me, were simply sharing elements of their sexuality journey. After all, that's how conversations work. First, you say something about yourself, then they share something about themselves, and so on.

So aren't these men simply relaying that they used bisexuality as a stepping-stone before realizing they were, in fact, gay?

Actually, no, that's not what's happening. These men are subtly dismissing my bisexuality. I know this because "I used to be bisexual" is always the *first* thing they say. It's then followed up with some nonsense of "When's the last time you had sex with a woman?" The point of this question is to invalidate my bisexuality because there's the possibility that I haven't had sex with a woman in a long time.

However, even if I hadn't had sex with a woman for years, or ever, for that matter, I would still be bisexual. Bisexuality isn't based on behaviors (that's why virgins and people in monogamous relationships are still bi). It's based on attraction and desire. Still, these naysayers attempt to use this faulty reasoning to somehow "prove" that I, a proud bisexual person, am not really bisexual. Honestly, I've noticed some gay men take a perverse glee in attempting to disprove my bisexuality through unsound logic.

But what truly infuriates me about the people who respond "I used to be bisexual" is their solipsist approach to sexuality. These men assume that their experience is the only valid experience. Since they used bisexuality as a pit stop to gay town, every bisexual man must be doing the same.

There are nearly eight billion people in the world, and at the risk of sounding like a kindergarten teacher, every single person is special and unique. So while many of our experiences mirror others', many do not. This is why you don't assume or project your own bullshit onto someone else.

It's also why I always respond to their microaggression with "You may not be bisexual, but I am, and I always will be."

EXPERT TAKE: The message conveyed here is that true bisexuality is not possible. The questioning of bisexuality as a legitimate identity has been identified as a significant microaggression. Just as Zachary says: while you may personally not be bisexual, it's important not to see that as evidence that everybody else is on the same journey you took. Remember, too, that just because someone is bisexual, it doesn't mean they owe you details of their dating history in casual conversation.

If you find yourself calling into question someone's self-expressed identity, it's best to acknowledge that they know themselves better than you know them and to accept that they are who they say they are.

"YOU DON'T LOOK GAY"

PHIL SAMBA

I HATE when people say this to me; it just makes me feel so uncomfortable. I struggled with my sexuality for so many years, so to hear that I don't look like the very thing that caused me so much distress in my teenage years and my early twenties is so annoying. When I was younger, the boys around me all wanted to be rappers, but I was more interested in singing. I felt like I couldn't say that out of fear of being shamed for not being exactly like everyone else. I also didn't express any femininity outside of my bedroom: I used to be really hyper and girly when I was alone but couldn't possibly be like that around anyone else. What I didn't realize was that I was also masking my ADHD alongside that feminine expression. It was like there were only two extremely binary ways of being a Black gay man: you must be either hypermasculine or hyperfeminine. There's nothing wrong with these, but I don't feel like I necessarily fit into these extremes.

> I'M A VERY MULTIFACETED PERSON;
> THE EXPERIENCES THAT I'VE HAD
> AND THE LIFE I'VE LIVED
> REFLECT THAT.

Being told I don't look, sound, or act gay is abhorrent as it is reinforcing the belief not only that Black gayness and Black masculinity are not mutually exclusive but also that there is something inherently wrong with me for being myself. Whenever I ask, "What does gay look like?" I'm always met with stereotypes of what said person believes I should behave as a gay man, most of which don't relate to me at all.

34

I'm not just a Black man, but I'm also a very tall Black man, which is perceived especially as me being intimidating, unemotional, and threatening when I'm nothing like this! I'm actually VERY emotional. For someone who spent so much time navigating these ridiculous, inapplicable stereotypes of being a Black man, I didn't expect to have to navigate even more ridiculous, inapplicable stereotypes of being a Black gay man. It was strange because everything that people wanted from me before was now the total opposite of what they wanted from me after I came out.

These preconceived notions also translate to the sex we have; men who are tops are considered and might even self-identify as being more masculine than men who are bottoms, although versatile men might be seen as more gender-balanced, transcending the gender roles that relate to identifying as a top or a bottom. The top's role is analogous to the seemingly "less gay" penetration role of a straight man in bed. I feel this belief can be even more prominent when considering Black men because of how historically we are often negatively represented as sexually aggressive and hypersexual, and are still seen this way in porn today.

I'm Black, I'm tall, I present masculine but not hypermasculine, and I'm gay, which is never considered a norm. I'm a very multifaceted person; the experiences that I've had and the life I've lived reflect that. I would love for there to be many more examples of multidimensional types of men who have decided on their brand of what masculinity is, showcasing that there are multiple ways to be a Black man. Honest visibility and positive representation are vital for boys who may feel displaced or like they don't belong for being themselves rather than someone else. I can relate to this. I know the excruciating split between who I was and who I was expected to be, and I found it very challenging to believe that I could be more than what I was always told I should be.

Black men shouldn't be chastised for moving away from the restrictive perimeters of what it means to be Black and what it means to be gay.

Perpetuating stereotypes tells us that pushing boundaries of expectations is wrong. Why is being like everyone else so important?

We have the agency and the freedom to rewrite our history, be whatever and whoever we want, make sure we are represented in the best possible way, and make a huge difference for younger Black queer men of the future.

EXPERT TAKE: As in many cases, this microaggression reflects the perpetrator's beliefs about stereotypes related to gay people. A humorous retort that can deflect this microaggression can be an opportunity to spark a discussion about such stereotypes. So, you can say something like, "Yes, you caught me...I'm trying to infiltrate straight society." This type of response can add some levity to the moment and make the perpetrator more receptive to becoming educated about the harmful impact of stereotypes and making assumptions about others. This can lead to the development of a more complex perspective.

ASSUMING A TRANS PERSON IS PROMISCUOUS

KO WILLS

*I*n my day-to-day life—at the grocery store, walking home, or even hiking—men will hit on me in a microaggressive way. Our society oversexualizes trans people—we see this the most in the media. This type of incorrect exposure leads to inappropriate behavior from men. Just because I'm a trans fem does not mean I'm seeking sexual attention or relations.

EXPERT TAKE: The assumption of sexual pathology or abnormality is a recurring microaggression that many transgender people encounter. The implication is that individuals who identify as transgender are constantly seeking sexual encounters. This microaggression serves to diminish the individual to nothing more than a sexual object. If someone commits this microaggression against you, your safety is the top concern; it might be best to avoid confronting them directly. To counteract the long-term effect of microaggressions like this, it is important to seek out support from others such as friends, family, or a counselor who can help you to process your experience.

"YOU'RE SO LUCKY HE STAYS WITH YOU, DESPITE YOU HAVING, ERR, HIV"

SUSAN COLE

*H*ere we go again. HIV is whispered, like the virus is listening out for the wake word and will spring into the speaker's vagina if it hears itself named. And me, as the hapless host of the virus, a creature to be pitied. And no matter how much of a dick the man I'm in a relationship with is, he is the glorious hero for being brave enough to stay with a woman with HIV. All this toxic microaggression delivered with lashings of saccharine sympathy and a coy head tilt. And I feel myself folding in, like stigma-fueled origami.

As a woman living with HIV, this has been my reality since diagnosis in the late 1990s. I had recently gotten married to my second ex-husband (I've had three so far, collected like stamps) when my diagnosis was delivered by a doctor who cheerily asserted, "The good news is you don't have syphilis; the bad news is you have HIV. And you have about seven years to live." Of course, his analysis of my life expectancy was ridiculously wrong, as people with HIV with access to treatment can expect to live as long as anyone else, but the trauma of my diagnosis lingered. And the comments from people I told were sometimes peppered with microaggressions, suggesting I should hang on to my husband as no one else would want me now. Despite the fact that I didn't "look like someone who had HIV," whatever the fuck that means.

Women with HIV regularly face these types of microaggressions, said cheerily with an alleged intention not to offend, but these comments, when heard enough, alongside the misinformation about HIV prevalent in society, can consume us, erode our self-confidence, and leave us hamstrung by self-stigma. Women living with HIV are more likely to be victims of domestic abuse, with abusers often telling their victims that no other man will want them, that they are unworthy, that if they leave, he'll tell everyone they have HIV, and they'll be shunned by others.

The microaggressions don't end there. We are regularly asked, "How did you get HIV?" It's no one's business, and many of us choose not to answer that question, but we see the rabid curiosity in their eyes. Blood transfusion? As a baby? Tick, worthy of sympathy. Through sex? Through drugs? Big red cross of disapproval and judgment for bringing it on ourselves. We're asked, "How long have you got?" The reality is with access to treatment we can expect to live as long as anyone else. Furthermore, if we're on effective treatment, it's impossible to pass on HIV through sex. Zero risk. Women with HIV can have babies born free of HIV. HIV isn't a barrier to us being able to do any job or living a long, fulfilling life. Yet HIV-related stigma continues to blight the lives of people living with HIV around the world.

But before you tilt your head in a sympathetic way, that's not my reality today. I may have HIV, but the virus does not define me, and the microaggressions I sometimes experience no longer have the power to diminish me. So, if I'm now told, "You're so lucky he stays with you, despite you having HIV," I'll look them in the eye and:

A. Tell then to fuck off. Or . . .

B. Tell them he's the one who is lucky to have ME.

EXPERT TAKE: It is important to educate oneself about someone else's situation before saying anything that puts them in an unfavorable light. And remember that just because you might know someone's HIV status, you are not entitled to any further information about their medical history. Instead of focusing on your perception of an HIV-positive person's relationship or asking them invasive questions, try to engage on things outside of their diagnosis—if they want to talk about their experience with HIV, they will let you know.

"I USUALLY LIKE VAGINAS AND GIRLS, BUT YOU'RE CUTE"

MARS ELLIOT WRIGHT

As a trans person dating, I am often baffled by people's frankness when mentioning genitals. I don't think cis people get asked specifics about their genitals as first messages on Hinge, but I have seen it across the board from cis women and men. It makes me feel like my humanity is completely out of the question until it can be boxed into an understandable binary. Like I do not deserve to be spoken to like a human until you understand in depth every part of my medical transition.

EXPERT TAKE: It is important to respect people's privacy in relation to their bodies. Considering someone only in terms of binary categories can be hurtful as well. Try to see someone in their full humanity rather than limiting or objectifying them or comparing them to other people you have been attracted to. In general, make sure the other person is comfortable with talking about something as personal and private as their anatomy before commenting on it.

ONLINE MICROAGGRESSIONS

GIGI GORGEOUS GETTY AND NATS GETTY

When we first started dating, we were hit with a tidal wave of negative comments and aggressive feedback, especially on social media. It was very jarring, and we never really sat down to discuss it. Gigi would have people questioning her transition, asking what the point was if she was going to end up with a woman, clearly mixing up the differences between her sexuality and gender. And Nats, when he chose to go public about his own transition, was bombarded with hate messages about how it was "a waste of time" and how this was the "worst decision of his life" if they were just going to be in a "straight" relationship.

People don't realize this wasn't a gender choice but a relationship choice, and we are still getting incredibly insensitive and aggressive comments from either people who are ignorant and don't want to try to understand or people who are clearly hurting themselves and taking it out on us since we are in the public eye and just trying to live out loud as the happily married couple that we are.

EXPERT TAKE: The microaggressions here can be understood as discomfort or disapproval toward transgender experiences. Making unsolicited comments online about someone's relationship solely based on their transgender identity is considered unnecessary and insensitive. So, if you are considering making online negative relationship comments toward a trans person, it may be beneficial to pause and reflect on your own potential biases and decide whether your comments would be beneficial or harmful to others. Ask yourself: What would your comment accomplish? Do you know this person's gender better than they know themselves?

"YOU'RE REALLY HANDSOME, FOR AN INDIAN GUY"

PRITESH SHAH

I start this by saying that I'm not a victim. I discuss this from a place of immense privilege I've experienced in my life.

After moving to Los Angeles, I started dating women from all different backgrounds and cultures. I was interested in expanding my own limitations when it came to connecting with someone. What I found interesting is that "You're really handsome for an Indian guy" was said to me more times than I can count. What I found funny at first turned into something I realized was stemming from ignorance, not malicious intentions. The most interesting part of this whole situation is that these women I was on dates with were trying to give me a real, genuine compliment. They had smiles on their faces, and I knew it took them courage to say it. That was the oddest part for me. I never corrected any of them. I usually laughed it off and kept the conversation moving.

Looking back, I would tell the old me that those conversations were worthy of a correction, even if it made the situation awkward. Also, if you're going to compliment someone, just don't end it with an asterisk.

EXPERT TAKE: The microaggression suggests that people from India are not typically attractive because they do not possess physical characteristics in line with Eurocentric standards of beauty. In situations like those Pritesh describes, the connection and attraction between the people on each side of the microaggression might facilitate a conversation. If you're comfortable with some light confrontation, it would be great to educate them and clarify the difference between intention and impact. One could say, "I appreciate that you think I'm handsome, but the way you said so didn't really come across as a compliment. Let me explain why."

"YOU HAVE A NICE DAD BOD"

SANDER JENNINGS

As someone who always promotes body positivity, I constantly receive comments about my body, shape, and size. It might come from someone who is trying to flirt with me. Or it might come from a friend trying to tell me that I look good. Since having a "dad bod" is something many people seem to compliment, I used to take it as one. I'd feel good when someone described me as filling in nicely and looking like a hot dad. It wasn't until I started receiving more hateful comments about my body that I realized that comments such as "dad bod" were microaggressions that didn't make me feel good.

Let me break it down. First off, for the large majority of my life, I always wanted a six-pack. I thought that if I had a six-pack, I would be happier. Despite working out five days a week for many years, I could never seem to get rid of some of my belly fat. Why? Because sometimes, genetics don't work in your favor, and I was making myself unhappy trying to get the six-pack. Once I started to focus more on staying fit instead of trying to get a six-pack, I thought that "dad bod" was the next best compliment I could receive. If I couldn't be the guy with the rock-hard abs, I wanted to have at least some sort of positive label. Once people started commenting things such as "You're not even in shape," "You've gotten chubby," and more, I realized that any direct comments comparing me to other people were microaggressions. I'm twenty-four and not a dad, and even if I was a dad, every dad comes in different shapes, sizes, and forms. Progress, goals, and genetics are different for everyone, so I no longer wanted to be compared to anyone else.

I SET MY GOALS
AND STANDARDS
FOR MYSELF.

Nowadays, for the most part, I try to acknowledge hate comments and microaggressions related to body positivity every few months. I recognize them as a way to educate my audience, encourage others, and show pride in myself because I know that my body is perfect in my unique way. Happiness comes from being comfortable in your own skin. That should always be more to you than getting a six-pack, meeting society's perception of a "dad body," or trying to meet any other mainstream idea about "the perfect body." I hope everyone can recognize that as long as you are remaining healthy and happy, then you should be confident and never let anyone put you down.

EXPERT TAKE: Here is another example of how comments about attributes that aren't necessarily subject to discrimination can still be profoundly othering. It's possible that the offender didn't mean to cause harm, but if they were to consider the difference between intent and effect, they could realize that their words were harmful. If you're comfortable confronting a potential romantic partner, try responding with something like, "I know you joke around a lot, but I actually find your comment about my dad bod to be hurtful." This can start a conversation about one's struggles with developing acceptance and pride in one's unique body type.

"YOU'RE SO
emotional."

BILLIE LEE

Years ago, when I owned and managed my own café in Los Angeles and needed to correct my employees on their mistakes, such as quality consistency and food safety, they would jump to a moment in which I expressed frustration and anger. Usually, the men would tell me that I was being too emotional: "Stop being so emotional," they'd say, or "You need to chill out." I even heard "Damn, boss, why are you so emotional when you don't even get a period?" Not only was I presenting as a woman, but I was in a position of power, and this was a dangerous way to undermine my authority: using my emotions to deflect from their bad behavior. At the time, I wasn't aware their behavior was a microaggression. It made me furious to be dismissed because I was a woman with authority correcting a man. Food safety was nothing to joke about, and to feel unseen and unheard was externally frustrating.

I heard this from men I dated, too, who knew I was on hormone therapy. When I disagreed with them about something, it was simply because I was emotional: "Are you taking too many hormones?"

I remember an argument I had with a previous partner about his dog. He would never take responsibility for his dog's bad behavior, and one day I walked into my room only to find my favorite pair of heels chewed to pieces. Of course, I was emotional. All he had to do was close my bedroom door, but he didn't take my feelings seriously. To him, I was just "too emotional."

The volume of these comments has only turned up over the years, and I know why. Traditional (read: dated, invalid) ideas of masculinity and femininity dictate that men are powerful if they show no emotion; similarly, when a woman shows emotion, it is because she is weak.

I *can* be emotional when I speak, but to use that as a negative both invalidates my feelings and implies that what I say doesn't hold value simply because I'm emotional when I say it. We must stop passing judgment on emotion. I'm passionate about what I do—about my work and my activism—which means I'm emotional about what I do. That's a good thing!

I used to feel bad for being emotional—like when I owned my café, the comments trying to control my emotions about something I felt so strongly about really affected me then—but not anymore. I'm proud of my emotions. I've learned through these microaggressions over the years that if my emotions come from a caring and loving place, then I have every right to express them. I'm also a double water sign in astrology, which means I'm sensitive to energy and very passionate. I wear it as a badge of honor.

So, yeah, I'm emotional about this. Why aren't you?

EXPERT TAKE: If you find yourself in a situation like that of Billie's employees, fight the urge to make your boss's comments about her gender and instead engage with the issue she's raising. Telling a woman that she is being too emotional in the workplace is not an appropriate way to raise a complaint. These microaggressions are often delivered as jokes, but they can cause real harm—and, of course, it's never okay to make comments about a coworker's gender or anatomy.

"YOU LOOK LIKE A REAL MAN"

Marquise Vilsón

As a trans masculine person, hearing things like "You look just like a real man" rubs me the wrong way. What does that even mean? Suggesting that I "appear" to be cis sends a message to me that cisness is supreme and my transness isn't valid without it.

I did not transition to be cis—I transitioned to be me.

EXPERT TAKE: This theme appears repeatedly throughout the book. Telling Marquise he looks like a "real man" is not a compliment but rather an invalidation of experience. Instead of comparing a trans person's appearance to that of a cisgender person, keep in mind that your opinion may invalidate their identity. If you want to compliment them, simply say it like you would to a cis person (e.g., you look great today).

"IF YOU'RE GONNA BE NONBINARY, BE HAIRLESS AND TEAR"

FRAN TIRADO

Honestly, some of the worst transphobia I might get on a weekly basis comes from other queer and trans people. Gay men don't see my gender and think my expression is some kind of gimmick. Others won't really validate my transness unless I medically transition or shave my mustache. So many trans women don't see gender-nonconforming people as trans. "If you're gonna be nonbinary, be hairless and tear" is one phrase I've heard before.

EXPERT TAKE: Sometimes, we experience microaggressions from people we think would be sensitive to our experience. Unfortunately, this is not always the case. If you feel safe responding, you can keep it simple, reminding the other person that gender expression is highly individual: "While that might be the case for you, it's not for me." Beyond the moment of the microaggression, it's essential to seek out validation and care from others who will understand and be sensitive to your own expression.

"I don't want to be seen as what others project onto me, but seen as my actual self."

—Mitchell Fahey

"YOU'RE TOO CUTE TO BE BLACK"

KAWASI WESTON

Since moving to Los Angeles, there is no secret that Black people are a minority. However, it seems things have gotten a lot worse, especially being an openly queer Black Man in Hollywood. Lately, there is not a day that goes by where I am not stopped or complimented for being a "Black Man" who is cute or sexy "to be Black." Just the other day, I was stopped by a "White Guy" and told that I was "the most attractive Black Guy" he had ever seen. The shocking thing is that he thought it was a compliment to me. I was so shaken by the phrase that I just walked away. To be placed in a beauty standard simply because of your race or the color of your skin is not only acting as a bigot but total and complete discrimination rooted in colorism and racism.

The old term was called "color struck." Which means to refer to people of African descent who have lighter complexion and/or European features as the epitome of beauty or desirability. This is not only toxic, but, I feel, extremely problematic because it attempts to directly remove the origins of beauty given to me by my Black mother, Black father, Black grandparents, and their Black parents. I feel that we are all beautiful and that more conversations need to be had on microaggressions, especially those built on the pillars of Eurocentric beauty standards.

If I had a chance to go back to that moment, I would have educated him on what he had done—in the hopes that he would consider how negative and divisive his comments had been. We must start addressing this type of behavior at its core.

EXPERT TAKE: The message conveyed here is that African Americans are typically not attractive, but Kawasi's lighter skin and European features render him good-looking. In response to this type of microaggression, you may want to shine a light on the comment through clarification. For example, in such a situation, you could ask, "Can you help me understand what you mean?" This type of response will allow the perpetrator to make explicit their intention in making the comment and could open a productive dialogue if you want to continue to engage.

CONCLUSION

NAVIGATING MICROAGGRESSIONS in dating and relationships can be particularly difficult. When you're out on a date or in a relationship with someone, the sting of discrimination can be especially painful. This chapter showed a variety of microaggressive themes, such as having one's identity called into question, people making assumptions about you without explanation,' being advised to "lighten up" in the face of offense, and being sexually objectified, among others. As observed throughout this chapter and elsewhere in this book, the offender's aim is frequently disguised as a compliment or making light of a comment (e.g., "I was joking") when they have committed a microaggression.

However, educating the individual and pointing out the inconsistency that what has occurred is actually offensive can go a long way. Dating scenarios occupy a sort of middle space between those with strangers and those with family. There's an opportunity to deepen your connection and learn from your mistake if you commit a microaggression against a romantic partner, and those on the receiving end may feel safer to address microaggressions with someone they're growing closer to.

If you're in a dating scenario and getting to know someone, try to target your praises toward something other than an identification group (for example, what they're wearing or the wonderful cuisine at the place they chose for dinner). If you are confronted with committing a microaggression, do not become defensive. Instead, take a minute to think about how you're feeling in the moment and apologize. Use the experience to help you grow and become more sensitive to and inclusive of others.

CHAPTER 3

Workplace

"YOU JUST NEED TO work harder.

Billie Lee

et's rewind to the years of Young Billie. The place? Los Angeles, City of Angels. I was a wide-eyed ingenue, having just moved from the corn country of the Midwest. I was still transitioning and had grown out my hair and dyed it a beautiful blond. I had gotten breasts and was feeling great!

One thing I needed to support my move was a job. No problem there—I had worked for years in both service and managerial positions since I was a teen in Indiana. My résumé was the bomb dot com. I just knew the perfect job was waiting for me to snag it. I sent out my résumé along with a pretransition headshot because I supposed this was LA, and headshots were basically everyone's business card. I was nervous sending my headshot of myself that I'd taken before starting hormones, but I didn't have the money to get new ones, so that had to work.

And wow, the calls came in—I was bombarded for in-person interview requests. *Knew it*, I smiled to myself.

Standing in my closet looking at interview outfit options, I felt a wave of panic wash over me when I realized that people would be seeing a totally different face from the headshot I'd sent them where I'd visually presented as male. Would that be an issue for them? Should I cut my hair or tape my boobs or something?

No, that's silly, I told myself. I had accrued so many years of experience in the service industry that they wouldn't care. I wouldn't hide my true self—I was proud of myself, and I was capable of any task an employer could put in front of me, no matter what I looked like.

Spoiler alert: apparently, it mattered. In interview after interview, I would show up in a professional outfit only to see the interviewer's face fall (even the same interviewer, mind you, who had said they wanted to hire me on the spot after seeing my résumé). Then I'd get an "Oh, um, we,

59

uh, just filled the position. Sorry about that." Or "Yeaaaah, we'll call you; thanks for coming in." Or even just a "Sorry, you're not for us." The ones that actually sat down with me when they had no intention of hiring me were the ones that hurt the most because it wasted my time. I was clearly fully capable of the job, but the interviewers' curiosity about my private life and transition kept us from exploring that. The ones that did give me the time of day were attracted to me as either some kind of fetish or some form of live entertainment. I remember one guy not hiring me but still reaching out for a "late-night drink at his house." I wasn't worthy of a job, but I was worthy of being his secret fetish? After a spate of these discouraging "interviews," I was distraught and depleted. Nobody wanted to hire me even with the wealth of experience I had and the clear vacancies available.

This was an incredibly painful time for me. I remember feeling so depleted, like there were undeniably ugly truths about my identity holding me back from getting a job. I had thoughts like, Was my choice to transition a mistake? How will I make money to survive? Where will I live if I can't get a job? Even worse: Why am I living in this pain when I could just end it all with suicide? With all these scary, fearful thoughts running through my mind, I couldn't help but have regret.

And one of the worst things about it was that the worst responses came from my friends.

"Girl, you've got this! All you have to do is just work a little harder!"

"Keep at it—you just have to put more time in!"

And so on and so forth.

What I needed was emotional support and help connecting me to people who would hire me. My friends meant well, but they missed what anyone who suffers this kind of discrimination needs: love, emotional support, and resources. I truly believe the one thing that saved me was not a job—it was an unexpected call from my father. He said, "Billie, I want you to know if you want me to walk you down the aisle someday at your wedding, and you're wearing a dress, I will." It was all the reassurance I needed in that moment of despair. His love and acceptance reminded me to keep going, to keep living my authentic truth. Still, to this day, when I'm doing press interviews, I always say hire us trans people—we deserve it. If you or anyone you know had the power to hire someone, please hire us.

So how, exactly, is this a microaggression? Telling someone to work harder when they fulfill—and go far beyond—any requirements needed to achieve a goal is a figurative slap in the face. I actually *didn't* need to work harder. Those who were on the hiring end weren't going to give me a job no matter what I did because I did not fit into their societal view of what "normal" looks like in a server.

Look, I've heard this kind of inspirational speech before—it's meant to encourage and uplift! But what it truly does is this: it invalidates the systemic injustices and discrimination that the recipient is facing while revealing the privileges that shield the speech giver from them.

EXPERT TAKE: In this very open and candid account, it is clear that Billie experienced transphobic discrimination when applying for a job. Not everyone can personally effect change around this particular type of workplace discrimination, but that means it's incredibly important for those who can. If you are in a position that involves making hiring decisions, it's vital to focus on the qualifications of a candidate over their appearance or identity—if your feelings change upon meeting a transgender candidate, for example, it's essential to interrogate that feeling within yourself. Within your organization, try to be mindful of how some of your own biases could impact your hiring practices. Offering training on implicit biases to individuals responsible for hiring is essential to mitigate these forms of microaggressions.

"*I WISH TO BE an individual, NOT A TOKEN OR A MIC for a community OF PEOPLE.*"

—Melania Luisa Marte

"... FOR A BLACK GUY"

FREDERICK JOSEPH

*T*here's a faint scar on my right knuckle: it's old, and most people can barely see it. In fact, there are days when I even forget it's there. But on other days, I can see it more clearly than any part of my body. Days when this scar is more familiar than my eyes, my lips, and most certainly my smile. When the memory of my glass-filled knuckle doesn't seem like a memory at all. When I am back in that room with blood flowing down my arm that seems to never run dry, as if being drawn from an endless well of harm.

Sometimes, our faintest scars tell the tales of our deepest pain.

Minutes after making this scar, I sat on a cold linoleum floor staring at shards of the mirror I had just broken, each piece reflecting fragments of a person I didn't recognize. A person who had spent his entire life hearing the phrase "... for a Black guy" as the bookend of countless statements that began seemingly positive. That phrase was attached to my existence so often I wouldn't have been surprised if someone confused it for my last name.

I had been "handsome," "kind," and "well-spoken" for a Black guy from nearly the first moment I had shared space with a white person. On its surface, some may call the phrase a microaggression, but at its core, it's a reductive stamp placed upon the existence of non-white people to remind us that we are just that—not white. An attempt to bolster the widely internalized and externalized racist belief that only white people are entitled to full humanity.

Thankfully, I had not internalized this belief, although in many ways, I had accepted it. Which was almost as bad. Because racist beliefs and systems are designed not only to treat you as inferior but to thin your soul until inferior becomes your normal.

But it didn't matter to me whether white people found me attractive, kind, or well-spoken. Those were judgments that mattered when you wanted to be desired. I hadn't worked as hard as I did in high school, undergrad, and grad school to be desired—I worked that hard to be *needed*. But I quickly learned that even if those with racist beliefs *need you*, it still doesn't mean they *respect you*. A lesson first taught a week after I graduated from business school. Upon receiving my MBA (Master of Business Administration), I was given the opportunity to interview for a role at one of the most prestigious marketing agencies in America, a place I had dreamed of working at for years. After my interview, there was no question in my mind that I had shown up more prepared and polished than any of my competitors. In fact, it was obvious based on the interactions with the three white people interviewing me that I was more prepared and polished than even them. I walked out confident that I had gained the respect I deserved and that I would likely be offered the opportunity I so badly wanted.

As I exited the office, I realized I forgot my favorite pen, so I headed back to retrieve it. As I walked up to the door of the room where I was interviewed, I overheard the voices of the white woman and two white men who had just interviewed me.

"Do you think he'd fit in?" one of the men asked.

"I'm not sure, but maybe," the other man responded. "I mean, he's smart, that's for sure," he continued.

"Yeah, he's smart—for a Black guy," the first man said matter-of-factly, as the other two laughed and made sounds of agreement.

In that moment, a pain washed over my body that felt as though all of the tears I was holding back had hardened into a lump in my throat. I hastily left the office, feeling like a crime had just been committed against my spirit.

That night, I found myself at home staring in my bathroom mirror at someone who felt destined to live a life weighed down by the judgments and gaze of people who would never allow me to be more than ". . . for a Black guy." People who would never allow me to be a human.

TO EXPRESS MY ANGER WOULD HAVE MADE ME THE VILLAIN, THE "DANGEROUS" BLACK MAN.

A lifetime's worth of fury and exhaustion introduced my fist to that mirror, and before I knew it, I was sitting on the floor surrounded by the crimson and glass proof of my pain.

In that moment, I found myself consumed by a fury that threatened to swallow me whole. And yet, I knew that showing this fury earlier to those who had wronged me would have only served to reinforce racist stereotypes. To express my anger would have made me the villain, the "dangerous" Black man that white society so often demonizes—even when we are rightfully angry. And yet, even speaking up calmly would have given up some of my power because I would have been extending my emotional and mental labor by explaining why what they did was wrong instead of mending the wound of what they did.

It is these sorts of double-edged swords, disguised as choices, that are so often left for Black people to decide how we want to confront a racist society. I opted to let my anguish out in a private moment and then heal my wounds—only to wonder when a similar moment would inevitably reopen them.

But something important happened on that cold blood-covered linoleum floor, staring at those mirror shards, besides releasing anger—I came to terms with truths. What was said about me after my interview was blatantly racist, but the beliefs of the people in that room were in many ways no different from the beliefs of the people who had seen me through a filter of racism when judging me as handsome, kind, or well-spoken. Simply put, the existence of microaggressions is still the existence of oppression.

As hard as we may try, marginalized people will never truly be respected by a society or its systems that see some people as less than human, whether subtly or blatantly. Which is why we must work to reimagine that society and dismantle those systems.

Sometimes, our faintest scars tell the tales of how our revolutions began.

EXPERT TAKE: The painful experience of racism cannot be overstated. Here we see again how our biases can impact hiring practices. The emotional impact of the statements made by the interview committee was devastating. Even in situations in which the candidate is not present, it is important to be self-critical and to reflect on our thoughts and the expression of those thoughts. Frederick is correct that society as a whole must change. We can start with our own situations, especially those in which we have power, such as when we participate in hiring committees in the workplace. If a colleague makes a comment like the one Frederick overheard, it's important to push back: not only are racist comments like these in a hiring context inappropriate but also the prejudice behind them may even be illegal.

"YOU KNOW SO MUCH FOR SOMEONE WHO IS UNEDUCATED"

Elisabet Velasquez

Six years after dropping out of high school at the age of sixteen, I obtained my GED. It was a proud moment for me, as not having a degree made it difficult to find employment or anyone to pay me a decent wage. During this time, I relied on social services to help me navigate things like medical care, housing, and financial security. Soon after obtaining my GED, I applied for and began working at a social service agency in the Bronx as a community follow-up worker. It felt serendipitous to be on the other side of social services helping people in a position that I was in just a few months prior. Like another kind of graduation.

A year later, I obtained a job as a case manager at another agency that assisted people with serious and persistent mental illnesses with access to care. Although a large percentage of our clients were BIPOC, the majority of the clinicians assigned to assess a client's need for care were white. This lack of diversity left me constantly having to explain culturally normative behavior that would otherwise be pathologized. I felt like I was the resident BIPOC whisperer.

One day, we conducted a home visit to a client whose cultural background I shared. The client talked fondly about her relationship with God, which included talking to God in the mornings and lighting candles for the dead. After the visit, my supervisor stated she was going to recommend that the client be evaluated for schizophrenia due to auditory hallucinations and religious delusions. My mother is, in fact, diagnosed with schizophrenia and is also extremely religious. Although it can be tricky sometimes, for the most part, I have been able to differentiate between the moments when she is having an episode and when she is simply practicing her faith.

I attempted to provide some insight on Puerto Rican cultural and religious practices and that speaking to God or the ancestors is not uncommon. My supervisor reiterated her belief that the client should be evaluated for possible schizophrenia. Being that I was new to the field and not a clinician, I decided that perhaps my supervisor's clinical expertise mattered more than my personal and cultural knowledge. I did, however, suggest that cultural competency training may be helpful for the organization as a whole.

Pathologizing BIPOC cultural values, religion, or communication styles is a subtle yet harmful microaggression that characterizes white culture values and speech as normal and those of BIPOC as abnormal. But that's another essay for another day.

My supervisor paused before she responded.

"You know so much for someone who is uneducated."

I froze. I couldn't understand how my education mattered in this context. She hadn't interviewed me for the job. How could she know my educational background? Had I mentioned having a GED before? When she sensed my discomfort, she tried to walk back her backhanded compliment.

"No, no, what I meant was you articulate really well. Look, my father is an uneducated man. He doesn't know how to read or write, and he's one of the smartest men I know."

I still didn't quite understand the comparison. Why wouldn't I articulate well?

"I'm sure you're aware that *I can* read and write," I responded.

"I see you're committed to misunderstanding me."

She went on to assure me that she meant no harm by calling me uneducated. Assuming my educational background was rooted in her unconscious bias that non-white people are educationally inferior.

The idea that Puerto Ricans are uneducated is not a new concept. Puerto Ricans have a long and complex relationship with education in the

United States. A political cartoon titled "School Begins," published in 1899, captures the start of this relationship. In this cartoon, Uncle Sam is poised as a teacher pointing a stick at four students. The students are all dark-skinned with unkempt hair, some only wearing socks; one child is barefoot. The children are sitting on a wooden pew, some slouched, their faces varied in expressions of fear, anger, and curiosity. They wear sashes around their waists that read: Philippines, Hawaii, Puerto Rico, Cuba. The cartoon references the expansion of US imperialism overseas. The caption reads: *Uncle Sam (to his new class in Civilization) Now, children, you've got to learn these lessons whether you want to or not! But just take a look at the class ahead of you, and remember that, in a little while, you will feel as glad to be here as they are!* Behind the four students are children reading books whose titles are representative of states previously acquired by the US: Texas, California, Alaska, New Mexico, and Arizona. These children are depicted as lighter-skinned; one young girl can be seen wearing shoes. They are well-groomed and poised in perfect posture. They are representative of a civilized society. Outside of the immediate classroom frame are stereotypical and racist depictions of Black, Indigenous, and Asian children, who are excluded from this educational process altogether.

The idea that non-white people are educationally inferior is a concept that predates this uncomfortable conversation with my supervisor and one that is rooted in the belief and implementation of the racial superiority clearly demonstrated in "School Begins" and that continues to live in classrooms and workplaces all over the United States today.

EXPERT TAKE: Telling Black, Indigenous, and people of color (BIPOC) they are "articulate" represents the microaggression of intellectual inferiority, implying that it is unusual for BIPOC to be impressive in terms of their knowledge, education, or intellectual skills. So before commenting on someone's level of intellectual ability in the workplace, even if you mean it as a compliment, it is important to consider the cultural context and to recognize that you may be harboring biases about a cultural group. This case also demonstrates the importance of increasing the diversity of employees in the workplace and highlights the need for employee training so they can be more culturally competent. Relying on one or two people in an organization to represent or explain nuances of an entire culture puts undue pressure upon those individuals.

"OH, YOU'RE THE MANAGER?"

RICHARDSON CHERY

*O*ftentimes when people ask to speak to the manager at this "fancy" place where I work, they never expect the general manager to be Black, so I always get, "Ohhh, you're the manager, can I speak to the general manager?"

I then proceed with, "Yes, I am."

It is always a shock to people that someone like me is running a place like "that"—the disappointment on their faces is obvious.

EXPERT TAKE: The underlying assumption conveyed here is that Black men do not—or should not—hold leadership roles in prestigious environments. The origin of the microaggression can be traced to the pervasive stereotype that Black people lack the necessary competence to occupy esteemed positions of authority. When you are in an establishment and someone tells you their role, take them at their word.

"DIVERSITY AND INCLUSION"

AKEEM OMAR ALI

*I*n today's job market, "diversity and inclusion"—or its lack thereof—has always been an issue. I've heard countless declarations throughout my experiences in job interviews about the importance of "diversity and inclusion initiatives." Sometimes, I've even been referred to company Instagram handles where they proudly showcase that one time they posted a black square in "solidarity." Yet, in every predominately white workplace I've found myself in, I've almost always been mistaken for another Black person on the team. In a perfect world, I'd be owed a bonus for every time I've been at the receiving end of such an "honest" or "simple mistake." I've been misnamed, mistaken, and misquoted in the workplace so often that it's impossible to not fantasize about some form of corporate reparations.

I never used to process these occurrences as microaggressions. I simply assumed they were, in fact, honest mistakes. They often didn't register on my cultural Richter scale as something I should be upset about. That is, until I was hit with a case of mistaken negro identity.

How is it possible for a human resources department to receive an email from one Black employee and then send their response to the wrong Black employee, with an entirely different name, when there's only two Black employees in the company? How racist does one have to be to read one name and think, "Nah, Gmail. You got it wrong. It's the other one"? The situation made me realize that these microaggressions were not minor hiccups but rather overt proof that they did not care about my individuality, nor were they interested in making me feel included. They hit their diversity quota, and that's all that mattered to them.

"We don't all look alike!" was the response I wanted to scream into the email chain. The irony is that I couldn't. Because then my actions would inevitably be viewed as "unprofessional" in comparison to the conduct of the perpetrator in HR. Black and Brown people are constantly forced to navigate double standards in environments like these. It feels like walking a tightrope between condescension and indifference. There is always a "Next time," or a "My bad," or "It's not that serious." The reality is that these failures of accountability do little to address and heal the constant blows these encounters deal to our psyches.

I'VE BEEN MISNAMED, MISTAKEN, AND MISQUOTED IN THE WORKPLACE SO OFTEN.

"Diversity and inclusion" is a phrase that these spaces love to use over and over and over again when recruiting new talent. They love to use these buzzwords whenever there is public outcry over the current social justice issue of the season. They use them internally at nearly every human resources meeting and in every digital communication. They even use it at luncheons. But unfortunately, it doesn't mean anything. Not really. The phrase rings as hollow as a black square on IG.

EXPERT TAKE: Tokenism in the workplace is an ongoing issue and unfortunately often experienced by BIPOC. It is considered an environmental microaggression because the lack of racial diversity within a workplace can be readily seen in daily face-to-face and online interactions as well as, for example, photos of employees on an organization's website. Perhaps the most egregious example of disrespect here is that Akeem was sent an email that was intended for the only other Black person in the workplace. It can be easy for people who commit microaggressions like these to write them off as honest mistakes, but they are a part of a larger pattern that we must reckon with. It is critical to make a sincere and committed effort to show respect for the individuality of our coworkers and not to treat anyone merely as an interchangeable member of a cultural group. All organizations need to take these types of microaggressions seriously as they can lead employees to become depressed, to disengage, and even, in some cases, to resign.

"YOU KNOW HOW YOU ARE"

Cornelius Jones Jr.

I was working for a prominent celeb creating and developing her fitness brand. A coworker crossed a personal boundary with me, and I spoke up for myself in that exact moment. During an employee review, the co-owner (a white male) of the company called me out as being an aggressor in that situation. His exact words: "You're unaware . . . You know how you are, you know that thing you do, how you can get sassy."

Protecting my emotional boundaries should never be judged or shunned, and the go-to word of "sassy" is a complete misrepresentation of Black people, Black women, and Black gay men; a misrepresentation of a person's authentic character; and a stereotype. We should be allowed to express when we are hurting, and emotions can be varied because experiencing hurt is complex and different for many. Black people shouldn't have to cover up feelings to avoid being labeled "difficult" or "hostile." Why are we held to different standards than others when we are experiencing emotions and dealing with trauma?

EXPERT TAKE: In the workplace, Black people are often looked upon unfavorably if they express any direct or firm emotion. It is important to allow people in the workplace to express their authentic selves without disparaging their character. This includes scenarios involving workplace conflict: when mediating or discussing situations like the one Cornelius describes, avoid charged descriptors like "sassy" and look at the entirety of the interaction rather than relating a Black employee's actions to stereotypes.

"Lighten Up!"

*I*n 2018, I owned a busy café in Los Angeles. I took a rundown bagel shop that looked like it was from an '80s sitcom and transformed it into a cute, cozy place my regulars quickly called home. I upgraded the quality of the food and added organic vegan items that become customer favorites. It was an amazing experience to create a safe place for people to visit, eat, and be themselves without fear of discrimination. My staff knew how important diversity and inclusion were in my personal life. I also made sure my staff was treated with the most respect from our customers; I did not tolerate disrespect.

I was protective of my busy little café. I wanted to succeed both for myself and for all of my customers who had become family to me.

When I would bring up important issues with my staff, troubleshooting or brainstorming on how we might improve our standards, I would constantly receive a "Lighten up, boss" from my kitchen staff before they'd return to whatever task they'd been dealing with before I'd entered the kitchen.

I was the owner of this café, and yet my staff members weren't listening to me whatsoever. Was it because I was a woman? Whatever it was, it caused me to feel unheard and not cared about. Not a great feeling! I had the responsibility of keeping my café open so that I could employ my workers so they could take care of their families. I felt a crushing responsibility to them and to the community I had built. My regulars used my café as a sanctuary to work, create art, and get away from their everyday hustle. People loved the way my café space felt, and I wanted to keep that going for them.

Maybe you've never owned a business, so here's another way in which you might get a "Lighten up!" lobbed at you.

One year, which happened to be during a presidential election, I took a trip to visit my family in Indiana. As we usually do when I visit, we gathered at a family member's house, and I would cook up something yummy and vegan to impress the fam. The conversation quickly went from "Wow, I can't believe this is vegan" to "Is Biden vegan?" Yikes. Political discussions in my family weren't usually fun. Even if they were about veganism.

TELLING SOMEONE TO "LIGHTEN UP" IS NOT ONLY DISMISSING THAT PERSON'S FEELING BUT ALSO INVALIDATING THEM.

Of course the subject matter of transgender rights came up, and a number of my family members piped up to tell me what was and wasn't appropriate for me to expect as a human right. When I tried explaining to my family how certain policies could severely harm me and my trans community, I received the inevitable "Lighten up, we're at a party." I quickly felt shamed, as if I had to strut lightly around my gender identity to make others feel comfortable.

Somehow, it was okay to debate and joke about these rights until someone who was actually going to be affected directly challenged them. Then, come on, just lighten up!

Whether you're discussing work matters, political or otherwise, telling someone to "lighten up" is not only dismissing that person's feelings but also invalidating them, making them feel like they are not seen or heard—effectively telling them that they and their beliefs simply don't matter.

A cousin of "Lighten up" is "It was just a joke!" When you feel yourself making either of these statements in a conversation, take a breath and pause for a moment. Think about why the person you're speaking to feels so passionate about what you're dismissing or joking about. Reset the conversation and be respectfully curious. If you are truly receptive, you might learn a thing or two. At the least, the person you're speaking to will feel heard.

EXPERT TAKE: To tell someone to "lighten up" is to imply that they are overly sensitive and that showing any sort of emotional reaction is unacceptable. These statements can make a person doubt their own experience and can be very harmful. In response to being told to "lighten up," it could be useful to bring the microaggression to the forefront of the person's awareness in a quiet moment. Try saying something like, "I know that you value everyone's opinions, so I wanted to share this with you: when you tell me to lighten up, it makes me feel frustrated and like my feelings aren't being taken seriously."

"ARE YOU CALLING ME A RACIST?"

CORNELIUS JONES JR.

This particular incident happened at a yoga studio where I was teaching. I requested a meeting with management because of a disagreement with my fellow coworker (a white female yoga teacher). She was microaggressive toward me from the day she joined the teaching staff. She would never greet or make eye contact with me but only spoke to me when my students would leave props or towels behind or when she needed to remind me of my timing. This triggered me because I felt policed, erased, unwanted, not valued, and unsafe as a Black man offering the practice of yoga in a predominantly white space occupied mainly by white women.

In a meeting about a particular exchange of words that she and I had with each other, she pushed the narrative that I became aggressive toward her verbally and physically. I called her out on the fallacy and inaccuracy of her statement and asked her to not use those words about me because they perpetuate a negative stereotype and narrative that has been placed on Black men in America for decades. She then began to cry and said, "Are you calling me a racist?" The meeting ended. I had enough of the hateful attack on my character. I left. She stayed behind playing into the role of the victim.

EXPERT TAKE: Oftentimes BIPOC experience being "invisible" or devalued in the workplace or, even, as in this case, being falsely accused of exhibiting aggressive behavior. If a Black coworker tells you that you have perpetrated a microaggression, it is important to pause, take stock of your feelings, and attempt to respond from a place of open-mindedness and compassion. The most advisable initial response may be to apologize; even if emotions are running high, try to recognize that your colleague is giving you an opportunity to defuse the situation. Moving forward, it's important to try to understand the other person's perspective on the interaction so that you can work on preventing any microaggressions in the future.

"WELL, ACTUALLY, I THINK . . ." INTERRUPTIONS

PRISCILLA BONNET

"*W*ell, actually, I think . . ." I can't even count the number of times my male coworkers interrupted me or talked over me, only to hear them later repeat the same exact idea I was trying to put forward. Women like myself experience this all the time—our ideas are ignored, then once a male colleague says it, it's finally heard.

EXPERT TAKE: The theme of invisibility is a pervasive experience for women in the workplace. The message conveyed is that a woman's words hold less significance than those of a man. If you find yourself in a situation like Priscilla's, it's fair game to interject and draw attention to the fact that you just said the very same thing. Or, if you happen to be a colleague who observes the male coworker interrupting or talking over Priscilla, it might be helpful to intervene by appealing to the microaggressor's values and principles.

For example, you could say something along the lines of, "I know you really care about having equal representation on this team, so I just wanted to point out that you talked over Priscilla when she was making her point. In the spirit of being open to all perspectives, I am interested in what she has to say." This approach brings her back into the conversation without creating conflict.

"AT LEAST YOU'RE MASCULINE"

R.K. RUSSELL

*O*ur society is obsessed with attacking femininity. Coming out as a professional football player in the NFL was the most challenging decision I had made in my life because of the deep-rooted homophobia and misogyny in male sports on all levels. Add in bisexual erasure from both the hetero and LGBTQ+ communities, and I felt at risk of losing everything I had worked my life to cultivate. If people weren't challenging my sexuality, they questioned my place in the sports world.

The sentiment I had heard from both communities was that at least I was masculine. They didn't care about my well-being, happiness, talent, or goals, only about my voice, body, tendencies, and mannerism, which I have little to no control over. They didn't care if I was happy, only that I was masculine.

EXPERT TAKE: Despite his bravery in sharing this aspect of his identity, R.K. was met with a response that left him feeling invalidated. The underlying notion of being told that "at least you're masculine" is not only that bisexuality is deviant but also that masculinity is a desirable trait for men and femininity is deemed unfavorable. In predominately male and straight fields like the NFL, the best way to show support for someone like R.K. is to affirm the entirety of their identity rather than praising the parts of them that most closely adhere to the status quo.

"SORRY, WE ONLY HAVE SALADS"

ZACH MIKO

When I first started modeling, the producers would sometimes apologize to me for the catering. "Sorry, we only have salads" was a common refrain. The assumption is that I could never be as big as I am if I ate healthy foods.

I have had a lifetime of disordered eating trying to "look healthy." People assume big people don't take care of themselves, but I promise I have tracked what I eat, how many calories I've burned, and how many points I've used closer than anyone you know.

EXPERT TAKE: It is very important to refrain from recommending "healthy" food options based on a person's size. The key in scenarios like this is to treat people the same way regardless of their size: there's no need to make personalized comments about the food options unless the person you're talking to has made a request.

"OH, I THOUGHT YOU WERE HOUSEKEEPING"

AWAKOKO

*A*s a nurse for thirteen years, you would think there's some level of respect, but unfortunately, that's not the case. As a Black nurse, I get overlooked by many family members and visitors who walk in and see me at the front desk: instead of asking me for help, they direct their questions at another person or someone walking in the hallway because they automatically assume I'm not a nurse and not competent enough to assist them. In reality, I'm in charge. When they're redirected back to me because I happen to be the one who can help them, I can see their discomfort and reluctance.

"Oh, I thought you were housekeeping . . ."

As a nurse, I get asked to empty trash cans and clean rooms more than giving medication and doing my actual nursing job because as a Black woman, I can't possibly be a nurse. The truth is Black women are educated, and Black women are indeed nurses.

What I get most from family members as a nurse for over thirteen years: "I'm sure Koko is a great nurse, but my mom is more comfortable with nurse Brittany."

The family's assumption that the color of my skin makes the patient uncomfortable is so hurtful to who I am as a human and a nurse.

EXPERT TAKE: The subtle yet impactful message conveyed through these microaggressions is that a Black woman does not have the necessary abilities or education level to fulfill the role of a nurse. The implication is that she must occupy a position of lesser status within the healthcare system. These assumptions are often made subconsciously, so it's important to be mindful when encountering staff members in any establishment. It can be as simple as taking a moment to observe the situation before jumping to conclusions about the person's role. For example, Awakoko is likely to be seen wearing scrubs or attending to patients. Noting these details is more helpful for everyone than using the color of her skin as shorthand for her role. However, even when taking these details into account, it is still a good idea to ask open-ended questions such as, "Are you able to help answer a question about a patient?" rather than making assumptions. After all, the person in question could be a doctor rather than a nurse.

"IT'S IN YOUR PEOPLE'S NATURE TO BE NURTURING"

MORGAN ELIZABETH

There was a time I had just finished executive producing a show and decided to not return for the next season. After several months I received a call from the other executive producer (a cisgender Caucasian woman) I had partnered with during my time in production. I was shocked to see her name come across my phone because we didn't exactly mesh during our time together.

After several minutes of niceties, she asked me to come back to the show as her personal nanny because she had seen how good I was with the children in our cast. She explained to me that the network was not being so nice to her about having her child on set, and she knew it was "in my people's nature to be naturally nurturing."

EXPERT TAKE: The impact of this microaggression is significant as it reflects the stereotype of Black women being seen as nurturing caretakers. This stereotype originated during slavery, when Black women would often be responsible for childcare and housework. The stereotype is still prevalent today. It was only in 2021 that the Aunt Jemima brand name was changed and the Aunt Jemima caricature removed from products. It is important to be mindful when making generalizations about the roles and activities of an entire group of people. Avoid the approach this former colleague took by taking into account the actual work that someone does—if you need a nanny, hire a nanny.

CONCLUSION

THE DAMAGING impact of workplace micro-aggressions cannot be overstated. It's been found that individuals who encounter microaggressions in their workplace tend to exhibit higher levels of job dissatisfaction, display lower levels of commitment toward their workplace, show symptoms of depression, and are more likely to quit their jobs. This is a serious concern since most of us need to work to survive!

This chapter sheds light on various microaggressions that are prevalent in the workplace, such as tokenism, invisibility, and intellectual inferiority. It is essential that all workplaces not restricted by anti-DEI legislation implement effective leadership initiatives in diversity, equity, and inclusion and provide adequate employee training to build awareness about implicit biases and the impact of microaggressions. These practices can aid in equitable recruitment, hiring, retention, and promotion practices. However, some states have recently enacted legislation banning workplace training on diversity, equity, and inclusion. Check the state law where your organization is based.

Workplace microaggressions are especially tricky for recipients to navigate since responding can result in retaliation or further discomfort for them. Therefore, it's especially important for bystanders to recognize microaggressions at work and to take care not to be part of the problem.

CHAPTER 4

Strangers and Acquaintances

"Wow,
YOU LOOK BETTER
Than Me
AND I'M A
Real Woman!"

Cisgender women—many of them my costars or fans of *Vanderpump Rules*—say this to me all the time. It might come from someone I meet for the first time in hair and makeup. Or maybe it's a fan who wants to take a photo with me. Whatever the circumstance, it's always presented like a gift on a platter. And in response, I tiptoe around it. I try to be kind and smile and thank the person because most people can be very defensive as if I'm the one that's being ridiculous or too sensitive.

As a people pleaser myself, I sometimes hate leaving people feeling bad even if they're in the wrong and my feelings are hurt. I've learned that's easier than sharing the hard truth that it makes me feel lesser than, as if I'm not real. It also puts me in mind of my trans sisters who may not present as traditionally femininely as I do. Does that make them even less than me? We *are* women, so what, exactly, is a "real woman"?

These microaggressions hit me hardest when I was filming *Vanderpump Rules*. My costars, boss, or someone else I cherished and looked up to would say things to me like, "I knew you weren't a real woman when I saw you down that beer" or "How is your voice so soft? It's usually the voice that gives it away" or "Is your hair real?" My cis costars and fans loved to pick out what was "real" about me and what wasn't. One of my costars could not get over the fact that I had real breasts and not implants at the time. She would say to people, "Look at her boobs. They're better than mine—how is that possible!?" She didn't believe me and wanted others to agree with her. My body was up for dissection on and off camera. I was the token trans, and they treated me as if I were an object rather than a person, taking me apart piece by piece. Being a celebrity was new to me, and it definitely brought on a lot of new challenges where the focus was on me; when you become a celebrity, you are looked at as more a character or a product of entertainment rather than a human with feelings. On a smaller scale, I remember this happening with my own family when I first transitioned.

At first, I didn't recognize these expressions as microaggressions because they were disguised so ingeniously as compliments. "How do you look like a real woman?" sounded in a blurry way like an affirmation of my femininity, a signal that I was inhabiting my womanhood well. But these "compliments" always felt off to me, too.

Why did these people feel the need to call this out? Did cis women go around telling one another, "Wow! You look like such a woman"? When I finally spoke with my trans community about it, I finally understood. I had my sister, the amazing Angelica Ross, over for tea, and I was telling her how amazed my other castmates acted around me and my transness. Angelica quickly and powerfully responded—it was amazing, they were suggesting, because I wasn't a *real* woman, I was playacting and had almost managed to fool them into thinking I was a woman. It was as if I was standing in a dark alley and the light turned on. I finally saw the ugly, scary truth. These people didn't see me as a real woman; their amazement wasn't a compliment.

Calling attention to these microaggressions isn't easy. I've found when I did speak up, people would think I'm being difficult or annoying, and it has cost me opportunities.

During my time filming *Vanderpump Rules*, I spoke up to my castmate Jax Taylor regarding this exact microaggression. I later found out I couldn't film with him anymore. I was hurt and confused because that season was Jax's and Brittany's wedding, and they were in almost all the major scenes, which meant most of my screen time was taken away. It was devastating to me and my mission as a trans woman. Visibility was the reason I signed up for that show, and that opportunity was taken away by one person who did not like me pointing out this very harmful microaggression.

Let's call these statements what they are: deeply hurtful insults, a harsh slap to the face that leaves red marks behind. And why have I stopped trying to correct people when they throw these unintended barbs at me? It's simple—the harm is always compounded when I do try to correct them, as I inevitably encounter defensiveness, a reprimand, a huffy response that, *actually*, that person was serving me a compliment. My boss at the time said, "Don't get your panties in a bunch. I'm only complimenting you, Billie." Then, annoyed, asked me to lighten up. See, people don't want to hear that their words are hurting me—they think it's actually *my* fault for feeling the way that I do. Being gaslit is the best way I can describe this feeling: people would rather convince you that you're wrong just to make sure they feel better about themselves or the situation. Eventually I felt like I was going crazy. I even went out of my way to avoid my boss. But after everything I've been through, knowing how happy and free I feel in this body, my true body—how can you tell me it's not real and then expect me to smile and say thank you?

EXPERT TAKE: While Billie's costars may have been intending to connect with her by drawing attention to common body parts or complimenting her by telling her that her mannerisms were like those of a cisgender woman, the impact was hurtful and alienating. If you want to give a compliment, base it on an attribute specific to that person, such as, "I like your hairstyle" or "That dress looks nice on you."

It's also important to listen to someone who might tell you they felt hurt or offended by what you've said. As we have seen throughout this book, microaggressions often occur unintentionally, so if somebody does bring one to your attention, just pause and listen to what that person has to say. It can go a long way to preserving the relationship.

"YOU'RE SO BRAVE FOR WEARING THAT"

Ko Wills

*I*magine this: I'm at an event chatting among friends, catching up, and talking about life, career, etc., and a lady introduces herself. As she is talking to everyone, I noticed her staring at me quite a bit. I ignore it and continue with my conversation. After a few minutes, the girl who had joined the group comes barging into our conversation. She looks me up and down and says, "Wow! You're so brave for showing your body like that! Good for you! You go, girl!" As if someone like me isn't supposed to show their body. Why did she feel obligated to single me out?

MY BODY SHOULDN'T BE UP FOR DISCUSSION.

After that, other people started to proceed with their personal comments about my outfit and/or my body. "Where do you get your confidence?" and "You remind me of Lizzo. She lets all her stuff hang out!" Stuff? Why is it that having my stomach and legs out is such a huge deal? There are plenty of girls tonight who are showing their "stuff." Why does someone who is plus-size have to be considered as letting it all hang out?

After that, it turned into a discussion on how liberating it must feel to be a plus-size model and putting it all out there like that. Then comments from everyone in the group started to roll in. "I just couldn't do that!" or "You're lucky you can eat anything you want and still model!" What does that even mean?

It's as if a body like mine is considered "unhealthy." I work out and enjoy physical activities. I don't just sit around and eat junk food all day. It is comments like these that make you feel as if you are different, less than others, and not worthy. It can make you feel as if you should just cover up to please others or even blend in so you won't be an issue. No one should ever be ashamed of their body. But society makes you feel as if being smaller is essentially better.

In situations like this, I try to of course respond politely and say things like "thank you" or even crack a funny joke to lighten the mood and not feel uncomfortable. I figure if I make them laugh, they won't focus on my body so much. The reality is I am completely uncomfortable. In my head, I'm thinking, "Why is my body such a discussion?" Why are the other women here being called "stunning" and "gorgeous," and I'm the brave one?

I look around at all the women beside me, and I naturally start comparing myself to them. They are showing just as much skin as I am. Some even more so, and yet I feel as if I'm basically naked in some sense. It's like it's outrageous to see someone comfortable with who they are and their body. Again, my body shouldn't be up for discussion. But it has now become the main topic of the conversation.

The issue of my body and being plus-size comes up for me in other microaggressions as well. For example, in preparation for that event, I had to go shopping and try on different clothes. Most of the time I like to go shopping with a few girlfriends. It's nice to get their opinions. We enter a store, and almost immediately, they are grabbing things left and right to try on.

I always start my journey off by seeing if the store has a plus-size section. Most of the time they do not, or if they do, the clothes are hideous. After that, I will search the other racks and try to see if there is something that catches my eye. Most of the time, I don't find my size on the racks. I then proceed to try to find the nearest employee and ask the question that I've probably asked now a thousand times in my life, "Do you happen to carry bigger sizes?" They then will proceed with saying things like, "Oh, sorry, we don't have bigger sizes in our store, but you should try online." Or another one of my favorites, "We don't have your size, but you should try the men's department—they generally run bigger."

Online? The men's department? Why couldn't I shop like my other girlfriends? Why is my size not available or only online and not in the store? Why do I have to go to the men's department in hopes I can find something that fits? These are the type of questions that would come up for me when these microaggressions would take place. It would make me feel less than others or as if I wasn't worthy of buying the same clothing as my friends.

All I can do is smile and say thank you. Or sometimes, I even say something funny like "Big girls need love, too" to not feel uncomfortable or show my disappointment. The employee would just laugh. Sometimes I would get a response where the employee would say, "Yeah, unfortunately, the bigger sizes don't sell as much as the regular sizes." As if that's supposed to make me feel any better. At the end of the day, I just want to be able to shop in a store just like my friends.

EXPERT TAKE: While the perpetrators may have intended to connect with and appreciate Ko as a plus-sized model, the actual result was that Ko felt hurt and uncomfortable. These kinds of microaggressions presuppose that persons with perceived "larger" body types are unusual; even comments that seemed like compliments to the people around Ko reinforce that othering.

It is crucial to remember that different body types are healthy and acceptable, and if you want to say something supportive at an event, it might be a good idea to focus on something specific the individual has done instead. In this scenario, you could compliment a specific outfit or mention something like, "Ko, I saw your recent magazine photos, and they looked great."

"I'M SURPRISED BY HOW GOOD YOUR ENGLISH IS"

STEPHANIE KWONG

I was speaking to a man at a Hollywood party, and he kept looking at me like I was an animal in a cage; he seemed perplexed and awed. When I finally asked him, "Is there something on my face?" his response was, "No, I'm just surprised by how good your English is." I was born in California, dude?! It made me feel small, hurt, and lesser; his words were, intentional or not, an attempt to alienate me from my own home, all because I wasn't white.

EXPERT TAKE: Unfortunately, this type of microaggression is frequently experienced by Asians and Asian Americans who are often seen as perpetual foreigners and not as "real" Americans. If you find yourself in a situation like this, and you feel comfortable enough to approach the conversation the way Stephanie did ("Is there something on my face?"), you can draw inspiration from her story: "Well, gee, I hope so—I was born in California." This type of response, while possible to deliver in a pleasant tone, makes the invisible visible and brings the microaggression to the forefront of the perpetrator's awareness.

GENDERED HONORIFICS

JACOB TOBIA

I will never forget the first time I saw myself mentioned in the *New York Times* as "Mx. Tobia." For months, I'd been speaking to a fashion journalist there who'd set out to write a story about nonbinary models but ended up realizing that he needed someone with something to *say*. So though I'm way too fucking ugly to ever *really* be fetishized by the fashion industry as a "model," he called me. Because he wanted to speak with a nonbinary person who didn't just inhabit the aesthetic but had the ability to compellingly communicate about it.

We first met for coffee at the Sunset Tower Hotel, one of the most iconic art deco buildings in the country, and trust me when I say I've never felt like a more glamorous girl. Me? A hairy, big-nosed nonbinary lady from suburban North Carolina? Being interviewed by the *New York Times*? In a historic hotel on the Sunset Strip? Pinch me, bitch.

For the next two months, I spoke with the journalist a handful of times, ultimately culminating in him and a photographer coming to my apartment to photograph me, then us traipsing over to the Los Angeles County Museum of Art to take some more photos. In typical "me" fashion, I didn't wear something expensive and designer for the shoot. I wore a skimpy turquoise and pink floral-print dress that I'd pulled from a bag of clothes my friend was getting rid of back in college, accessorized with necklaces I'd gotten from my best friend Deanna's grandma and a fifteen-dollar purse shaped like a cat.

When the story finally came out, it felt a little out of body. I was the *entire* cover image of the *New York Times* Style section above the fold. In the paper of record, I was referred to as "Mx. Tobia." And at first, it felt like recognition. I don't even remember them asking whether to use the gender-neutral honorific; I think they just did it because that's what their style guide recommends for nonbinary people. Or maybe I *had* asked them to? Who knows. Either way—for a fleeting moment, seeing myself referred to as "Mx. Tobia" in the *Times* made me feel seen.

But then I read the article, which characterized me quite shadily as "a fast-talking Instagram phenom with a penchant for rainbow lipstick, face-filter selfies and post-academic theory-speak." Ah yes, those silly nonbinary people. Always talking too fast. Always posing and posting on Instagram. Always wearing gaudy, over-the-top lipstick. Always filtering their faces. Always communicating in theory-speak. (I'm a Southern lady, born and raised. I know passive-aggressive insults when I see them.)

I DEMAND YOU TREAT EVERYONE EQUALLY.

At the time, I was proud of being referred to as Mx. Tobia. But these days, four years after the article came out, I find the whole thing so tiring. Why does the *New York Times* continue to insist on outmoded, stodgy, stuffy honorifics in the first place? Most publications have done away with a "Mrs.," "Ms.," "Mr.," and "Mx." altogether. But the *NYT* has clung onto a system that forces each person quoted in the paper to be classified within an archaic, gender- and marital-status-based form of reference.

Why must women quoted in the *Times* still be subjected to the debasing idea that their marital status has anything to do with *anything*? Why force people to be classified as either "Ms." or "Mrs." when you can just refer to them by name? Why must nonbinary people quoted in the *Times* be forced to draw such attention to our gender by using the often-unseen honorific "Mx."?

These days, I don't want to be referred to with honorifics at all. Don't call me Mr. Tobia. Don't call me Mx. Tobia. Just call me Tobia, or Jacob.

Keep my gender out of it. Stop employing, and then continuing to force me into, a system that was never built to accommodate me (or any woman who bucks at the idea of having her marital status incorporated into how she is named) in the first place.

And while we're at it: if you're going to continue insisting on using such archaic language, then I demand you treat everyone equally. Create a distinction between unmarried men and married men, too. Make it such that "Mr." means he's married and "M." means he's single.

Because as it stands, "Mr." tells me nothing about whether or not he's available or on the market. And trust me, this nonbinary hottie needs to *know*.

EXPERT TAKE: It is critical that we refrain from making assumptions about someone's gender identity, pronouns, age, or titles. Jacob raises a good point when they question why we need to employ gendered honorifics at all! In situations like Jacob's, the reporter should have asked what honorific they preferred; in most cases outside of the *New York Times*, though, it's often best to forgo those titles entirely.

If you are in a conversation and someone uses a gender honorific that is incongruent with your identity, you can say (or write), "I understand that you meant to be inclusive, but I don't use Mx. before my name." If, unlike Jacob, you do have a preferred title, it's of course appropriate to share it.

INTERSECTING MICROAGGRESSIONS

Rain Valdez

When I first moved to Los Angeles at the age of nineteen, I didn't know very many people. So when strangers would ask me where I'm from, I'd say, "I grew up on Guam, but I was born in the Philippines." Growing up on Guam, there was never really anything special about me except for maybe that, standing at 5'9", I was taller than most local islanders. And when I say nothing special, I mean that it was pretty normal to speak the way I did and look the way I did because I was surrounded by my people. But in Los Angeles, I found myself constantly being exoticized. The question that I would learn to anticipate would soon follow me for the rest of my life is . . . "Where are you *from*?"

BECAUSE I'M ASIAN, I THINK PEOPLE ASSUME I'M SUBSERVIENT.

In my early twenties, I found myself reveling in the "specialness" that I soon became. My olive skin, long brown hair, and svelte physique deemed me modelesque and exotic to my local Angeleno counterparts. I felt different. Like a unicorn. Even gorgeous! Which most would soon adopt as a way to describe me, but after a while the interrogation of my ethnicity and background got very old very quickly. Especially after learning that most Americans don't know much about Guam or the Philippines. They seemed to not have learned much about it in school. Which I found very odd considering that on Guam, American history is a huge part of the curriculum and our relationship with the US and Guam's position in the

South Pacific are a huge part of why Guam is an American territory and why we have one of the biggest American military bases in the world. A crucial detail that seemed to have been completely forgotten.

I remember trying to explain this to a white cisgender woman in my acting class after she asked me where I was from (of course!) and then proceeded to reduce me to a joke and made me feel very small. Of course I laughed it off and even added a self-deprecating response . . . "I know, right?! Like, who would ever be from Guam?!"

The joke was a hit and everybody laughed. I wasn't sure if they were laughing at me or with me. But I knew one thing: I said it to make them feel comfortable about making me feel small. That moment was so painful and became a vivid memory that I ended up writing it in my web series *Razor Tongue*.

As I got older, these microaggressions would eventually start to make me feel uneasy. Men were very quick to sexualize me or patronize me to the point where in a few of my relationships, I learned that I was nothing but a prize. A life-size statue that was won and is only there to look very pretty and exotic. Though fortunately, my "exoticness" and "gorgeousness" would also help me land some very important jobs in my life. I was smart about it and used it to my advantage. Or so I thought. What I learned was I was mainly hired as the bad guy. And being a pretty woman would soften the bad news to some very important clients. I was reduced to a puppet that my white cisgender bosses would know exactly what to do with. They weaponized my femininity and exoticness to their own advantage.

Even though by title I had a decent position, I never had any power. One time, at the same job, we all had to drive somewhere for a client meeting. I had offered to drive, and one of my bosses made a remark about not wanting to die going to lunch! When I asked, "Why would you think you would die?" Another one of my white superiors chimed in and said, "Well, c'mon, Asians are bad drivers!" It was said in such a matter-of-fact way with a little bit of humor that I surprisingly agreed! When in reality, I'm actually a good driver and was also deemed a "good driver" by DMV standards. A few years later, this same stereotype would eventually be perpetuated by a man I would be in a relationship with. But at that point, I was over it and learned to stand up for myself. I did not immediately agree.

Because I'm Asian and pretty, I think people assume that I'm subservient and that they can get away with treating me like I'm below them. And while I'm grateful for my privileges and the spaces I get to occupy, my gratitude is often mistaken for contentment. Because I *should* be grateful, any sense of self-expression and desires of my own suddenly equates to audacity or worse—difficulty.

But the truth is these microaggressions were never really about me. It's about them and their lack of ability to recognize a multicultural world that we live in. It's their resistance in accepting that the world they live in and the people in it aren't there to be in service to them. But to find our own path and make our own lives as we see fit. Now that I'm older, microaggressions don't bother me as much. Instead, it reminds me of a dying system that was designed to make me feel small and powerless. It reminds me of my innocence and how much I was willing to participate in my own oppression just to fit in. But today, I'm a seasoned powerhouse creative who knows how to navigate a world not built for her. I'm an independent, proud Asian American transgender woman who knows how to speak for myself, honor my innocence, and allow my light to shine around the people I love. And because of that, I can now find healing in being able to empathize with who I used to be.

EXPERT TAKE: The types of microaggressions experienced by Rain happen far too often to Asians and Asian Americans. Stereotypes, like those about Asian women being subservient or Asians being bad drivers, are hurtful outright, but even questions like "Where are you from?" that feel innocuous to the people asking can be harmful over time.

In response to these types of microaggressions, you can keep it simple—Rain did what felt right for her in the moment, but it's okay if you don't want to make jokes in response or call attention to the microaggression: "I grew up in Guam and now live in LA" is a totally sufficient answer. If you feel comfortable with more confrontation, it may be helpful to challenge the stereotype embedded in the microaggression. Again, you can keep it simple if you like: "That's a negative stereotype about Asians."

"I'LL PRAY FOR YOU"

JOCELYN MONDRAGON-ROSAS

grew up believing that praying is a way to show love to each other. While I didn't do it often, I did pray for my family to be safe and to have good days.

It wasn't until college that I realized that praying for others meant "curing," and I didn't understand why strangers needed to pray for me to be "cured" when they didn't know me.

Once in college, I was on my way to visit my college advisor for next year's class scheduling when a stranger stopped me and asked if they could pray for me to walk. I was in disbelief partly because I've never been prayed by others to walk and also because it was the most random interruption to my day. They took my wheelchair as a sign that I couldn't walk when in actuality, I'm an ambulatory wheelchair user, which means that I can walk. Now, praying for others isn't inherently bad. It's the intention and the assumption behind the prayer when you walk up to a person with a disability.

Do you know people with disabilities? Do you know their disability or illness? Do you know their religion or if they even have one?

These aren't questions that most people ask themselves when they're praying.

For example, if I were to pray for my mom, I would pray for her to be safe on the road. I pray for her safety because I know she drives to work every day. However, the very act of walking up to a stranger with a disability and saying to them "I'll pray for you" is making an assumption about their disability and life. With that said, why did this person with the disability immediately draw you to pray for them? The honest answer is that you felt bad or pitiful seeing them.

I ask that before you pray for a stranger with a disability, you examine why you want to pray for them in the first place. Maybe then you'll see that you're not really praying for their goodness of heart but rather for yours. If you really wanted to extend a prayer, you could ask, "Is it all right if I pray with you?" And if they say yes, you could then ask them what they would like their prayer to be about. Otherwise, why would you pray for a person that you don't know anything about?

EXPERT TAKE: It is important for us to not make assumptions about people who use wheelchairs. Because Jocelyn was in a wheelchair, the stranger assumed that she could not walk (like many people who use mobility devices, she can). Also, it was assumed that she would appreciate being prayed for without knowing anything about her religious or spiritual background. The message conveyed within these microaggressions is that it's sad and pitiful to be disabled and that having the ability to walk is preferred, so Jocelyn needs to be "healed."

Even though the person who stated they would pray for her likely meant it as a comforting remark, the impact of such a microaggression is experienced as condescending and invalidating. Thus, before making a remark to a person whom you might perceive as "disabled," it is important to reflect on what you are attempting to do when you start such a conversation. You can still get to know someone and connect without focusing on their ability status.

ASSUMING A PERSON OF COLOR
IS A SERVICE WORKER

JESSICA MARIE GARCIA

J was taking groceries out of my car, and a woman in my neighborhood approached me and asked if I was a home care worker. I had to tell her no; this was my house, and I lived there. Because of how I looked, there was no way this could be my home. I had to work for someone who lived here. Single moments like these aren't life-changing, but they add up and always remind me that I'm different.

EXPERT TAKE: This microaggression reflects the stereotype that Latinx women always occupy lower social classes; it revealed a perhaps unconscious belief that a person of color didn't belong in the neighborhood unless it was to work for a presumably wealthier, white homeowner.

Jessica's simple response is all you need to use in a situation like this; however, if you feel comfortable, you can ask the perpetrator to consider the microaggression by replying, "Oh, no, this is my home. Not all people of color are home care workers." In all cases where you choose to reply directly to the perpetrator, it is important to consider the context, especially when that person is a stranger to you. If the tone of the other person feels hostile, take care of yourself first and foremost.

Compliment or Microaggression?

"YOU'RE SO WELL-SPOKEN"

EXPERT TAKE: This type of microaggression reflects the same sentiment as experienced by Frederick Joseph and Elisabet Velasquez in the "Workplace" chapter. Telling a Black person that they are well-spoken is not a compliment, and in fact, it is experienced as an insult. It is important for the recipient of such a microaggression to choose whether or how they might respond to the perpetrator based on the context. If you're comfortable confronting someone who commits this microaggression, you can keep it simple: "I think you meant to compliment me, but I experienced your comment to be insulting."

"TO ADDRESS MY *Vernacular* is <u>not</u> a compliment. BLACK PEOPLE <u>do</u> SPEAK WELL. *Period.* NO SPECTACLE NEEDS TO BE MADE."

—MARQUISE VILSÓN

"YOU DON'T LOOK PERUVIAN"

Enrique Chiabra

When I first moved to the US, some people would say, "You don't look Peruvian" or "You are too tall to be Peruvian." As a teenager, I didn't think much of it, but now I can see how that was a microaggression because they were assuming that all Peruvians had to look the same.

I still get those comments (here and there), and I reply by saying that Peru is a very diverse country and that it is wrong to stereotype an entire country by looks.

A few years ago, I was shopping for furniture, and the lady who was helping me said, "I love your accent, where are you from?" I didn't mind the "compliment" and replied I was born in Peru. Then a few minutes later, she asked me if I had just moved here. That was very uncomfortable. On the way home, I asked my boyfriend if my accent was really that bad (haha). I was clearly taken aback, offended, and upset. Maybe this lady thought she was complimenting me, but in fact, she was perpetrating a microaggression.

EXPERT TAKE: The message conveyed is that all Peruvians look the same based on stereotypes. It is presumed that all people in the "outgroup" share the same experience (or appearance in this instance). It is important to consider that just because someone is from a particular country does not mean they have the same experience as someone else you know or reflect common stereotypes. So before commenting on how someone from a different country compares to others from that country, pause and reflect to decide whether your comment would benefit the person or your relationship. If you are attempting to connect with someone from elsewhere, you can ask more open-ended questions that aren't focused on how well they fit your expectations of people from other places (accents, physical appearance, etc.). Try something like, "How would you compare living in Peru to the US?" Finally, Enrique was upset by the microaggression that assumed he had not been in the US very long because of his accent. It is critical to note that calling attention to someone's accent, as indicated here, can make them feel like an outsider who does not belong. It is best to refrain from making assumptions about how long someone has been living in a country based on their accent.

"YOU LOOK JEWISH"

JEREMIAH RIPLEY

I've been told I "look" Jewish my whole life. Most of the time when people say "You look Jewish," they aren't meaning it as a compliment. I was at a friend's birthday party in Los Angeles where I was mingling with the guests, most of whom I didn't know. When a woman walked up to me with a deadpan facial expression and asked, "Are you Jewish?" I deflected by using my go-to phrase, "I'm Jew . . . ish." She looked at me confused and said, "Knew it." As she gave me the up and down, she said, "I just looked at you and thought . . . Jewish," her face looking like she had smelled something rotten.

Her somewhat innocent observation is part of bigger anti-Semitic stereotype Jewish people deal with all the time. Minimizing the experience of an entire ethnoreligious group to physical characteristics. There is no one way to look Jewish. There is no one way to be Jewish.

EXPERT TAKE: It is important to be mindful that biases can be conveyed through our words and even gestures (including looks), as in this instance. It is essential for people to become acquainted with any anti-Semitic feelings they may hold. While it is challenging for us to admit to any negative biases we may hold toward others, remaining in a state of unawareness of our unconscious or implicit biases increases our chances they may be communicated as microaggressions. Try to catch yourself before speaking if you find yourself speculating about a stranger's cultural or ethnic background: it's unlikely to come across well.

"YOU'RE FAT, SO YOU MUST NOT WORK OUT"

KO WILLS

I often get questionable looks at the gym. During one of my favorite workout classes, the teacher once assumed I couldn't do some of the exercises, and without asking, they would demonstrate modifications in front of the entire class, leaving me embarrassed and ashamed.

The thing is plus-size people like me do work out. We not only work out, but we're also strong and just as capable as anyone else.

EXPERT TAKE: The message conveyed is that because of Ko's body size, she could not perform the exercises as originally intended without making them easier. Unlike some random encounters with strangers, the relationship between a gym client and a teacher can allow for a more direct response—the teacher, after all, wants to facilitate the workout experience, and this is useful information for them. In a situation like Ko's, try something like, "I know you mean to be helpful here, but showing me these exercises with modifications makes inaccurate assumptions about my abilities." This direct response lets the perpetrator know what you need, but it also invites them to reflect on their assumptions on their own.

"WHAT ARE YOU?"

JESSE MONTANA

rowing up in Montana was a bittersweet, humble beginning especially being queer and second-generation Asian American. Identity was always so confusing for me growing up in a city that was predominately white and heterosexual, dating girls and guys, being in the closet, and navigating through the continuous struggle of finding where I fit into all those spectrums. Being multiracial, having a Vietnamese mother and a French Polynesian Filipino father, only added to my identity crisis. The most common questions were always within the first couple minutes of meeting someone: "So where are you from? What are you?" or "So are you Indian? Chinese? Japanese, Spanish, Native American?"

I'm proud of my journey of self-discovery and acceptance through all this because although it wasn't easy at the moment, I now have a blessed opportunity to amplify my voice for not only multiracial Asian Americans but also my LGBTQ+ family. We are all different on so many levels, but love will always win.

EXPERT TAKE: It is important to approach each person we meet with a genuine desire to get to know them and all of their complexity. Speculating about a stranger's or acquaintance's background is usually not advised, but reducing Jesse to a "what" even further dehumanizes him. So, when you meet someone and really want to get to know them better, it's advisable to focus on their interests—it will provide you with more information than their country of origin anyway.

"OH, WOW. YOU'RE TRANS? I COULDN'T TELL"

JESSE MEDINA

Them: "Oh wow, you're trans[gender]? I couldn't tell."

Me: ". . ."

Sigh. The good ol' "I couldn't tell" response. If I had a dollar for every time I've heard this, well, you know the rest.

Intent versus impact. I'm pretty sure it's safe to say that the person behind this response intended this to be a positive one. However, it doesn't negate the fact that the impact of this response isn't a positive one.

When I receive this particular response, one (or all) of three things occur:

A. I am immediately reminded of the not-so-pleasant beginning stages of my transition.

B. I immediately am saddened at the thought that it's 2022, and trans people still are dealing with microaggressions such as this one.

C. And/or me being viewed as a man diminishes, and an investigation or examination involving my body parts and my private life begins.

The funny thing is every time I make an attempt to let people know that their choice of words is harmful, I end up becoming the one at fault. Like, how dare I (the actual person affected by this language) have the audacity to not accept this "compliment" with open arms? How dare I inform people that this response, in fact, is not affirming or validating in any way? Some nerve I have, huh?

Just so that we are on the same page here, everyone's trans journey looks and means something different to them—it's nonlinear. Period. A response such as "I couldn't tell" isn't a compliment. In fact, it's a reminder that there is some sort of made-up (and messed-up) criteria as to what a trans person should and ought to look like, therefore implying that there was a time that *you could tell*—whatever that means.

EXPERT TAKE: As Jesse aptly puts it here, there is intention versus impact. While the person making the comment here may have intended to give Jesse a compliment, the impact was one of invalidation. Jesse's experience is similar to Billie's at the beginning of this chapter. Whenever you intend to give a compliment and the response doesn't go as expected, it is important to not be defensive and to listen carefully to what the recipient of the intended compliment has to say. It will cost you nothing to simply apologize and move on.

"ARE YOU . . . LOST?"

OMKARI L. WILLIAMS

I was waiting to meet a friend for lunch. He was in from out of town and staying at the Waldorf. It was pouring rain, and I was in jeans, a yellow rain slicker, and rain boots. I was sitting in the lobby reading as I waited and then noticed that the security guard was eyeing me. Eventually he came over and asked me what I was doing. I replied that I was waiting to meet a friend, and then the penny dropped. I said, "You think I'm a hooker, don't you?" He was clearly uncomfortable saying yes. I looked him dead in the eye and said, "Dressed like this, I'd starve," and went back to my book.

Don't let the snappy response minimize the damage of this exchange. It was decades ago, and I can still feel the heat in my body as, once again, I had to justify taking up space in a place that not only wasn't built for me but was built to exclude people who look like me. Belonging is a human need. Being told that you don't belong and trying to prove that you do can destroy your soul. In addition to the normal challenges of life, you're fighting to prove your worth, your humanity. That Black people have survived and thrived in this country is a testament to our resilience, our resourcefulness, our intelligence, and our refusal to let a racist system tell us who we are and who we can be.

EXPERT TAKE: It is important not to make assumptions or generalizations about one individual based on stereotypes. In a scenario like this, the security guard did not need to engage— Omkari was simply reading, not usually an activity that requires intervention from hotel security. Upon seeing a Black individual who was dressed casually, however, this person assumed that she could not be affiliated with anyone in an upper-class establishment such as the Waldorf and therefore she must be a sex worker. This example underscores the importance of increasing one's self-awareness (see resources at the end of this book).

CONCERN TROLLING

KEAH BROWN

*O*ften, the thing that I find most interesting about people who do what I call "concern trolling"—which is when strangers ask you a question about your health or well-being in a way that is both ableist and invasive—is that when you call them out on it, they try their best to backtrack and insist that they are a victim of my "inability" to see that they are just concerned about me.

Beyond the regular standard racism, like being followed around in stores or asked to show my receipts when my white counterparts don't have to do the same, being visible online means that I am often the subject of concern trolls. They ask me to prove that I'm disabled and ignore my every boundary about offering me cures for my disability because my existence in the world or on the internet makes them so uncomfortable that they feel the need to have to fix me. Because they hate the idea that I don't need to be fixed at all.

They don't believe that I could possibly be happy like this. I am happy like this.

EXPERT TAKE: Expressing empathy or concern for someone you know who may be in need of care is what makes us human. However, when interacting with people online whom you do not know, offering cures or asking someone to justify their ability status is hurtful and offensive. It is inadvisable to offer your unsolicited remarks or opinions to a stranger online with the intent to "fix" them.

"I'M SO OCD."

I was diagnosed with a mild case of obsessive-compulsive disorder (OCD) when I was a child. I remember feeling the breath catch in my throat and stopping everything I was doing at the time, regardless of how important it was, to step back and forth over a stick twelve times because I knew that was the only way that I could save my family from dying in a house fire.

So, I truly do know the weight of having OCD, of having to flip a light switch a certain number of times before leaving the house, say, or aligning the cans and jars in the pantry just so. It can be completely debilitating to one's life. I was consumed with my compulsive thoughts. They even kept me awake at night as I would go from room to room, constantly checking to see if my family was still breathing. After missing weeks of school because I was so worried my family's house would burn down because they kept things plugged in, my family finally admitted me to a psychologist where I was diagnosed with OCD. My therapist gave me great exercises to battle the compulsive thoughts, and as I matured out of childhood, I also grew out of my OCD.

However, it still lingered in my teens and as I started dating. I remember my first love—oh, how that relationship triggered my OCD. He was a wonderful, trustworthy person, but my compulsive disorder convinced me otherwise. I would measure his lotion bottles to make sure he wasn't masturbating, or I would sneak around and count his condoms and smell the sheets. No matter what I had to do, it was compulsive, and even though it was no longer life or death like it was when I was a child, it was still a must to relax my mind. I quickly got back into therapy, begging my therapist to help me answer, "Is this what love is like for me now?!" It took time to control those compulsive thoughts, and I worked hard with my therapist. As I grew out of my teens into adulthood, I could function more easily in everyday life, which was amazing; however, I failed to leave one thing behind: my ease around using the phrase "OCD." It can be so easy to drop it casually in conversation.

"Girl, I'm *so* OCD when [insert something I would say about cleaning my apartment or organizing my closet or sanitizing my kitchen]." I used to be ashamed of my diagnosis that I wouldn't tell anyone, and then over time as I grew out of my disorder, I noticed people using it as a slang or badge of honor as if the disorder was a positive personality trait. At first I thought, *Oh, I can use it now because it's something people brag about.* But I didn't realize the harm until I remembered my own painful journey with OCD as a child.

I still feel my skin prickle and get hot when thinking about a particular time in which I used the term OCD carelessly.

When I was younger, looking for a job to support myself while I honed my skills as an artist, I found myself in an interview for a food service job.

The interviewer looked down the bridge of their nose at me and asked me to describe my organizational skills in a few words.

Easy enough, right? I opened my mouth and out spewed—

"Oh! Yes, I'm incredibly OCD about neatness and blah, blah, cringe, cringe, blah."

The interviewer sat up suddenly in her chair, giving me a warm smile.

"Oh, you have OCD? I actually do, too!"

I wanted to melt into a puddle right then and there. I had just carelessly flung out a mental health disorder to describe my state of cleanliness.

How many other words in the dictionary exist to describe such a thing? I'll tell you: a lot.

You never have to resort to using "OCD" to describe a particular trait or the amount of attention you devote to something.

Luckily, the interviewer moved on to other questions fairly quickly, and to the best of my knowledge, I didn't do her harm, but it could have just as easily been the opposite. Simply because I had exerted a lack of care around my word choice. I wish I had spoken up with an apology and stood firm in my correction that day, especially knowing how painful OCD can be. She and everyone else struggling with that disorder deserve better.

So I'm here to offer you a clichéd phrase—but one that holds meaning: think before you speak.

EXPERT TAKE: Having a mental health disorder can be very challenging, and we may not know that someone we just met has one. Even for someone like Billie, who herself lived with obsessive-compulsive disorder in her youth, it can be easy to conflate neurotypical traits like a desire for neatness with symptoms of OCD. While the interviewer Billie spoke to brushed the moment off, pervasive comments like this can be harmful and invalidating, especially as they continue over time.

If you experience this type of microaggression, it can be useful to indicate to the perpetrator that they have said something offensive—and you can do this without disclosing anything about your own history if you prefer. For example, a response here could be, "I know you probably meant to use the term OCD as a substitute for neatness, but it may be difficult for some people to hear." This way, you are suggesting to them how this type of microaggression can be perceived.

The most important thing, though, is to take care of yourself. If you experience negative thoughts about yourself after the incident, it is important to seek help from a trusted friend or counselor to process your feelings around the microaggression.

"YOU LOOK SO EXOTIC"

SJ SINDU

I once entered an elevator at work in Illinois with a white man in a suit who said loudly, "Namaste!" I nodded politely and scooted to the corner, avoiding eye contact. I know how this goes. Unfortunately, it was a slow elevator. "Where are you from?" he asked. "Boston," I said, knowing full well what would come next. "No, I mean originally." Of course. I ignored him, hoping he'd get the hint. "You look so exotic," he said. "India? Why didn't you respond when I said 'Namaste'?" Thankfully, the elevator reached my floor, and I hurried out.

This same exchange happens regularly with different strange men, all of whom seem to think that tokenizing and exoticizing me is the way to forge a connection.

A number of them have even asked, within the first thirty seconds of meeting me, if I would cook for them. I've been called "exotic," "spicy," "fiery," and one time, a man even said, "I bet you're curry-flavored." Several unrelated men have ended their brief, racist courtships by asking, "Are you pledged to some Indian man you don't know? You don't have to marry him. I'll take care of you."

EXPERT TAKE: The first encounter SJ describes is more upsetting than it may seem on the surface: to be in an enclosed space as a stranger escalates from an ill-advised greeting to a growing barrage of questions and personal comments is deeply uncomfortable. Her further experience of being asked if she is "curry-flavored" represents the theme of sexual objectification experienced by Asian Americans. Being objectified in this way sends a debasing and threatening message to the target. Microaggressions based on sexual objectification, whether deliberate or not, have the impact of imposing power and dominance.

Again, assessment of safety is important if one is in a potentially threatening situation with a perpetrator. SJ did not feel comfortable engaging in the discussion in the first scenario and instead waited until she could leave the situation. This is a totally acceptable reaction: microaggression recipients owe nothing to the perpetrator. If you do not feel threatened, then interrupting and redirecting the conversation by saying something like "Please stop that type of talk" sends the message that what was said was unacceptable and will not be tolerated.

"WHO ARE YOU HERE TO SEE?"

JOÉL LEON

*W*ell, this one was right around the time of Trayvon. I was caught in the rain waiting outside this very beautiful mansion-type building in Brooklyn. I had a studio session to record for. I rang the buzzer, and while I waited, a white woman came to me after exiting the building and asked me who I was there to see. I mentioned the name, and fortunately, my friend had come immediately after. But the thing about dealing with microaggressions as a Black man is you don't have the luxury of discerning whether or not someone is simply asking you a question or if they're judging you based on your skin color.

EXPERT TAKE: The message communicated by the question is that he, as a person of color, did not belong at an upper-class location. As mentioned here, there are many instances where one is left wondering if a microaggression occurred or not. This process of mental gymnastics can leave people feeling emotionally depleted and drained of energy. Thus, it is important to be aware that asking a person to justify their belonging in a location may be based on bias. It's possible that the woman in this scenario was trying to be helpful, but unless someone seems in distress, it's often best to leave them to it. So, if you find yourself in this situation, pause and reflect to discern where your question might be coming from.

"HOW TALL ARE YOU?"

ZACH MIKO

I always knew I was bigger than the other kids, but when my fifth-grade teacher used me as an example of what a giant is while teaching Norse mythology, I learned I wasn't the same. It's rare to walk into a new space without being asked how tall I am. Though it seems like an innocent question, it was never asked of my friends of average or shorter height.

When a stranger asks, "How tall are you?" what they are really saying is "You aren't normal."

Like with the giants of myth, "normal"-sized people view my very existence with subconscious curiosity, trepidation, and fear. Thousands of years of legends and lore have set people of size apart from their average-sized counterparts, and so a disconnect has been hardwired into our everyday lives.

Would you ever ask an average-sized stranger how tall they are or how much they weigh? You would never, because it is rude, and you know the average-sized person may feel self-conscious or insecure about those numbers. But the same consideration for humanity isn't given to people on the extremes of the size spectrum. We're often less as fellow humans and more as circus curiosities.

As a man, because large size is conflated with strength and physical ability, you're made to feel like you should never complain about your height because other men may be envious of you. But I'm not here to intimidate people; I want to be accepted, and I want to be one of the group, a member of society. It took me many years to find comfort in my size, and the only way to do it was to take my self-value out of the hands of strangers.

WHY ARE YOU SO SENSITIVE?

EXPERT TAKE: Even when you exhibit traits that are considered positive (like being a tall man), it can be very uncomfortable when others' comments cause you to feel objectified. In such cases, it may be good to just let them know in a sincere and earnest way that when people focus on your height in ways that suggest you are different from others, it makes you feel uncomfortable, and you would rather not make that the focus of discussion. If you aren't up for that level of directness, try deflecting: "I get asked about my height a lot! It's not the most interesting thing about me, though, I promise."

ASSUMING WE SHARE AN IDENTITY

MITCHELL FAHEY

As a white, cisgender, straight-passing man, I always feel like white, cis, straight men assume I'm just like them when they discuss certain opinions regarding race, gender, sexuality, etc. This incorrect labeling by these intolerant people frustrates and saddens me to no end. I don't want to be seen as what others project onto me but seen as my actual self as a demi/pansexual, open-minded, kind-hearted, Jewish Aquarius who wants to see everybody be treated with love, care, and respect.

EXPERT TAKE: Everybody has their own unique background, beliefs, and behavior. Never assume that someone is the same as you just because you notice some similarities to yourself. The old adage "Don't judge a book by its cover" is still relevant in the modern world. Take time to really get to know someone before coming to conclusions about who they are.

"BLACK ATHLETES ARE ALL BRAWN AND NO BRAIN"

R.K. RUSSELL

I remember college professors and coaches alike being shocked at how articulate I was, as if being a student-athlete was only for show and a prerequisite to being dim and dull. Now intelligence, smarts, and being able to score high on standardized tests do not make someone dumb, smart, worthy, or worthless. But I was more upset that none of my white teammates who played the same sport and got similar grades as me never got the same shock when they spoke. What about athletics and Blackness makes people feel the need to stereotype my intelligence or, even more so, my dialect?

EXPERT TAKE: This microaggression is predicated on the negative stereotypes that Black people are intellectually inferior. Responding to microaggressions can be difficult, especially when they come from those in positions of authority, as in this example. If you are familiar with that individual, you may say, "You seem surprised by my articulateness. Would you mind telling me why?" It's also crucial to take care of yourself and talk about your feelings with others who have had similar experiences.

ALWAYS A SUSPECT

CEDRICK WILEY

*T*ire of going to stores being followed by staff. I understand the unfortunate stereotypes of POC. It doesn't make it any less infuriating for staff to assume I'm there to shoplift.

EXPERT TAKE: Cedrick talks about being followed in stores as if he were about to shoplift. This microaggression is founded on the negative expectation that Black people are poor and will steal. The message is that he is a thief who cannot be trusted. It is critical to question one's beliefs about criminality based on race and to avoid engaging in mistrust-inducing behaviors.

POLICING A BLACK WOMAN

MELANIA LUISA MARTE

There's the older man at the airport who can't fathom that I am able to afford a first-class seat on the same flight as his main-cabin seat. He is visibly annoyed and insists on asking what "group" I am in, as if knowing the truth will pacify the idea of what "group" he feels I belong to. A group that he wishes did not coexist in the same world as his. The grouping of things and people keeps these aggressive experiences in a constant loop.

It's the man who is not a person of color insisting on referring to me as a person of color as if those were my pronouns. As a Black woman, I say "such and such." He says, "So as a woman of color, do you believe . . ." I believe I wish to be an individual, not a token or a mic for a community of people who will never be the monolith others wish us to be. I wonder, then, is he just person or person of no color? Or human adjacent to the human of color? Is he the noun and am I the asterisk?

It's the woman at the grocery store who taps my shoulder to remind me that the freshest fruit can always be found at the back of the food display as she watches me shop. Or the other woman who can't keep her hands off my freshly braided hair. She says my hair and I are "oh so beautiful." And I do feel beautiful. Beautiful and awfully policed.

They all happen to have a particular agenda and presumption about my status and life that feels as if they wish to unravel the puzzle that is my existence, my skin color, my hair, my culture. And sometimes I bite back, but lately, I smile a big, bright smile, and I continue on with my day. And in that tiny revolution, I am reminding myself and them that I do not exist for their entertainment.

EXPERT TAKE: Melania endures microaggressions that indicate second-class citizenship, objectification, and tokenism. She was thought to be lower class when asked what "group" she belonged to at the airport. She was also instructed by a woman at the grocery store that the freshest fruit is in the back. These microaggressions suggest she is neither wealthy nor educated enough to shop for food knowledgeably. In such a situation, it may be best to look out for yourself: say thank you, if it feels safest, and that you were aware of this fact already. You can then ask, "If you don't mind my asking, what about me made you think I wasn't aware of this?"

Touching her braids, on the other hand, is an invasion of her personal space that objectifies her. The other person views her as simply a thing she can touch. In response to this form of microaggression, it's fine to reply, "No, you cannot touch my hair" if asked and to step back and tell them to stop if they do. There's no need to educate the other person if this happens to you: prioritize getting your personal space back, and take care of yourself.

CONCLUSION

CONTRIBUTORS IN this chapter discuss their own encounters with microaggressions, both from strangers and from people they know, in a variety of settings, from parties to simply walking down the street. Some of the topics explored in this chapter include expressions of surprise or disgust, assumptions of social class status, attempts to "fix" persons with a perceived disability, comments about physical size, and presumption of criminal activity, to name a few. And, as we can see, there were attempts to connect and get to know someone by delivering "compliments," such as when Billie was informed she looked like a "real" woman or Kawasi was "too cute" to be Black. While the intentions were good, the effect on the recipients was seen as damaging and invalidating.

When we are tempted to compliment someone based on their race, ethnicity, or gender identity, we must pause and consider whether the comment we are about to make would be useful. Instead, when we're trying to get to know someone and want to compliment them, it may be best to focus on features connected to a shared interest or other attributes (e.g., "That looks great on you" or "I really enjoyed reading what you wrote"). And, if you are the recipient of a microaggression from a stranger or acquaintance, it can be beneficial to utilize strategies that retain your dignity, bring the microaggression to the perpetrator's attention, and use that moment to educate the offender. However, if your comfort or safety is a concern, it may be wiser to do nothing and go on. Not all microaggressions can or should be addressed in the moment. As usual, it is critical to take care of yourself physically as well as psychologically.

ON SAFETY

BRIAN MICHAEL SMITH

I wanted to share my experiences of microaggressions to help others understand their impact, but every time I tried to write, my mind went blank. I realized I had developed a defense mechanism that prevented me from registering all the belittling, insulting, and dismissive behavior I faced daily. Even if I had the emotional capacity to withstand them all, I would spend my entire day addressing them. When I sat down to recall a specific microaggression, I became conscious of the negative space that carves out my existence as a Black trans man in this country, and the tightness and heat I felt were rage that I had no place to put. Describing a microaggression would be like describing a thread in the rope around my neck. Instead, I would rather keep it loose and wear it as a scarf.

HOW TO RESPOND TO MICROAGGRESSIONS

Dr. Gina C. Torino

Here are a few strategies that you can use after a microaggression has occurred.

- Take a deep breath, reflect on your feelings, and attempt to remain nondefensive.
- Be thoughtful, empathetic, and matter-of-fact when discussing an incident.
- Look upon the incident as an opportunity for education and improvement.

WHEN YOU EXPERIENCE A MICROAGGRESSION:

AFTER THE INCIDENT

- Pause, tune in to your feelings, and attempt to respond without counterattacking.
- Prioritize safety. If needed, interrupt, redirect, or disengage temporarily.
- Request a private discussion to avoid public defensiveness.
- Focus on intention vs. impact (e.g., "I know you may have meant it as a joke, but what you said was hurtful to me.").
- Connect the act or comment with a stereotype by "making the invisible visible" (e.g., "Not all Asians are good at math.").

AFTER THE CONVERSATION

- Process the incident with supportive friends and allies.
- Build a support system of culturally competent friends, allies, mentors, and community groups.
- Report the incident to a supervisor or HR if ongoing microaggressions are experienced in the workplace.

WHEN YOU WITNESS A MICROAGGRESSION:

AFTER THE INCIDENT

- Be an ally and validate the recipient while still recognizing the perpetrator's dignity.

CHECK IN WITH THE RECIPIENT

- Check with the recipient privately and offer to assist in further talking with the perpetrator.
- Offer to talk one-on-one with the perpetrator about the incident.
- If in a position of authority, consider mediating a dialogue between both parties.

IF SPEAKING WITH THE PERPETRATOR

- Highlight what the perpetrator has in common with the recipient.
- Contradict stereotypes by presenting personally known counter-examples.

WHEN YOU COMMIT A MICROAGGRESSION:

WHEN CONFRONTED

- Do not respond defensively. Listen and be open-minded.
- Acknowledge the impact without requiring the recipient to explain.
- Accept responsibility and genuinely apologize for the microaggression.

AFTER THE CONVERSATION

- Reflect on the microaggression's origin in unconscious bias and work to prevent further incidents.
- Commit to self-improvement (e.g., make use of publications and online resources to educate yourself).

RESOURCES

In this section, you will find tools that will aid you on your journey toward greater self-awareness, assist you in preventing and responding to microaggressions, and support you in coping with the potentially harmful psychological impact of microaggressions.

READINGS:

Banaji, Mahzarin R., and Anthony G. Greenwald. 2013. *Blindspot: Hidden Biases of Good People*. Random House Publishing Group.

> This book explores the science of implicit biases and what people can do to change them.

Kendi, Ibram X. 2019. *How to Be an Antiracist*. Random House Publishing Group.

> Explores the manifestation of racism and how one can go about becoming antiracist.

Yabut Nadal, Kevin L. 2023. *Dismantling Everyday Discrimination: Microaggressions toward LGBTQ People*. 2nd ed. American Psychological Association.

> Explores LGBTQ microaggressions, their effects on mental health, and how mental health clinicians can help clients cope.

Yabut Nadal, Kevin L. "A Guide to Responding to Microaggressions." CUNY Forum 2, no. 1 (2014): 71–76.

> Provides guidance on how to navigate situations where you might be either the recipient or the perpetrator of a microaggression.

DiAngelo, Robin J. 2018. *White Fragility: Why It's so Hard for White People to Talk about Racism*. Beacon Press.

> Investigates in-depth how white fragility arises, how it perpetuates racial inequities, and what we can do to change.

Sue, Derald W., Christina M. Capodilupo, Gina C. Torino, Jennifer M. Bucceri, Aiesha M. B. Holder, Kevin L. Nadal, and Marta Esquilin. "Racial Microaggressions in Everyday Life: Implications for Clinical Practice." *American Psychologist* 62, no. 4 (2007): 271–86.
> This seminal article provides the first microaggression taxonomy as well as the initial set of themes from the literature.

Sue, Derald W., Cassandra Z. Calle, Narolyn Mendez, Sarah Alsaidi, and Elizabeth Glaeser. 2020. *Microintervention Strategies: What You Can Do to Disarm and Dismantle Individual and Systemic Racism and Bias.* 1st ed. Wiley.
> Provides tactics on how to intervene on the personal, organizational, and societal levels.

Sue, Derald W., and Lisa Spanierman. 2020. *Microaggressions in Everyday Life: Race, Gender, and Sexual Orientation.* 1st ed. Wiley.
> Expansive and in-depth look at the manifestation and impact of microaggressions.

Gina C. Torino, David P. Rivera, Chrstina M. Capodilupo, and Kevin L. Nadal, Derald W. Sue. 2018. *Microaggression Theory: Influence and Implications.* 1st ed. Wiley.
> Explores scholarship and research related to all forms of microaggressions.

Wilkerson, Isabel. 2020. *Caste: The Origins of Our Discontents.* Random House.
> Examines the concealed caste system in the United States and focuses on its adverse consequences.

VIDEOS:

Disclosure (2020). Featured on Netflix, this eye-opening documentary shows Sam Feder, Amy Scholder, and Laverne Cox discussing the influence of media portrayals of transgender persons on individuals.

Not Your Model Minority (2022). In this thirty-minute documentary, Jon Osaki shows how the Model Minority Myth about Asian Americans has divided communities of color and explores ways to fight structural racism in America. https://www.newday.com/films/not-your-model-minority.

The Color of Fear (1994). This documentary, directed by Lee Mun Wah, features a group of eight men of color discussing the state of race in the US. The video chronicles raw and emotional disclosures about their experiences of race and racism. The outcome is a deeper understanding and trust. Although many of us may be apprehensive about engaging in such discussions, we can hope conversations like these will take place at some point in our lives. https://www.imdb.com/title/tt0484384.

A Class Divided (PBS Frontline) (1985). This is an excellent, classic video that demonstrates how quickly and easily children learn prejudice and discrimination. Very powerful film. https://www.pbs.org/wgbh/frontline/documentary/class-divided.

Passing (2015). This short documentary feature follows three trans men of color as they examine the intersectionality of race, gender, and identity, as well as the challenges that are brought about with multiple marginalized identities.

Peanut Butter, Jelly, and Racism (2016). This brief, two-minute segment by Saleem Reshamwala from the *New York Times* unpacks important dimensions of implicit bias.

In *How Racism Makes Us Sick* (2016). David R. Williams discusses how unconscious bias, residential segregation, and negative stereotypes can lead to negative health outcomes for people of color. https://www.ted.com/talks/david_r_williams_how_racism_makes_us_sick.

Microaggressions in the Classroom (2019). Producer Dr. Yolanda Flores Niemann highlights high school student experiences with microaggressions in the classroom. https://www.pbslearningmedia.org/resource/cb19-ss-microaggressions/microaggressions-in-the-classroom.

When Reality TV Meets Transgender Representation (2019). This *Vice* video special features the author of this book, Billie Lee. In this video, Billie shares her experiences of being a trans woman on reality TV as well as the lessons she gained from them. It explores intentions, assumptions, and impact.

Responding to Microaggressions (2020). This short, two-and-a-half minute video by the Wisconsin Technical College System provides tips on how to respond to microaggressions when they happen. https://www.youtube.com/watch?v=HrCgBLoMxTQ.

ONLINE TOOLS, EDUCATIONAL EXPERIENCES, AND ACTIVISM:

Project Implicit. To better understand the implicit biases that shape our thoughts, decisions, and actions, a group of scientists collaborated on a project called Project Implicit. Take a test to find out more about yourself: https://www.projectimplicit.net.

Undoing Racism: The People's Institute for Survival and Beyond. This sponsors workshops that promote growth and self-discovery by diving deep into exploring how society has shaped thoughts and beliefs about race. https://pisab.org.

Southern Poverty Law Center (SPLC). The SPLC works with communities to end white supremacy, develop intersectional movements, and promote human rights in the South and beyond. https://www.splcenter.org.

PFLAG. PFLAG is the biggest nonprofit in the United States committed to supporting, teaching, and advocating for LGBTQ+ individuals and their allies. https://pflag.org.

Stop AAPI Hate. This organization is the main anti–Asian American and Pacific Islander hate incident collector. It involves reviewing data to figure out what is occurring where, and to whom, and advocating for resources that offer successful options for resolution. https://stopaapihate.org.

Avoiding Microaggressions in Classrooms and Online. This resource will help you learn more about how to identify and respond effectively to microaggressions in educational and online platforms. https://collegeeducated.com/resources/avoiding-microaggressions-in-classrooms-and-online.

National Equity Project. This organization's goal is to improve the lives of marginalized children and families. Great tip sheet on how to respond to microaggressions: https://www.nationalequityproject.org/responding-to-microaggressions-and-unconscious-bias.

Center for the Study of White American Culture. Offers ongoing online workshops on decentering whiteness and building antiracistcist, multiracial communities. https://cswac.org.

Human Rights Campaign. The Human Rights Campaign wants LGBTQ+ people to live freely and with equal rights. The foundation has useful resources on health equity, laws and legislation, hate crimes, and more. https://www.thehrcfoundation.org.

UnidosUS. Through research, policy analysis, and state and national advocacy, UnidosUS has served Latino communities since 1968. https://unidosus.org.

Radical in Progress. This site offers self-study guides that promote self-awareness and social justice. https://www.radicalinprogress.org.

American Civil Liberties Union (ACLU). Works to defend and promote racial justice, women's rights, trans rights, and more. https://www.aclu.org.

PODCASTS:

Intersectionality Matters with Kimberlé Crenshaw (African American Policy Forum). Kimberlé Crenshaw, a legal scholar, activist, and lecturer who developed the theory of "intersectionality," hosts this podcast that provides insightful and informed discussion of issues faced by Black women.

Code Switch (NPR). Hosted by Shereen Marisol MerajI and Gene Demby, *Code Switch* is a popular race and identity podcast. Since 2016, the hosts have covered Black gun ownership, Hawaiian language revival, hip-hop, mass incarceration, how to talk about racism with kids, and Indigenous nations' treaty rights.

Gayish. Gayish is an award-winning podcast that debunks one gay stereotype each week. It has been featured in *Buzzfeed, Oprah Magazine, Esquire,* and *Queerty.* Mike and Kyle approach themes like the hanky code, sadness, and open relationships with levity, honesty, and irreverence.

Gender Reveal. Gender Reveal is a nonbinary and transgender podcast. Listen to interviews from famous trans people, evaluate current events, and learn more about gender.

Self-Evident: Asian America's Stories. This podcast is hosted by James Beard Award–winning journalist Cathy Erway and effectively depicts Asian American life through recorded narratives, personal anecdotes, and community conversations. Since 2019, *Self-Evident* has challenged tough identity questions and unpacked AAPI communities' unique challenges.

MENTAL HEALTH RESOURCES:

988: Suicide & Life Crisis Lifeline. If you experience suicidal thoughts and need help, dial 988 in the US. The lifeline provides information for you or your loved ones in times of crisis as well as twenty-four-hour, free, and confidential support for those who are in crisis. https://988lifeline.org.

Substance Abuse and Mental Health Services Administration (SAMHSA). Also known as the Treatment Referral Routing Service, the national helpline's number is 1-800-662-HELP (4357) and is a confidential, free, twenty-four seven, 365-day-a-year information service in English and Spanish for people with mental and substance use disorders and their families. This service refers to local treatment centers, support groups, and community organizations. You can also text your zip code to 435748 to locate help nearby. https://www.samhsa.gov.

LOCATE ONLINE THERAPISTS THROUGH:

https://www.psychologytoday.com/us/therapists/online-counseling
https://www.betterhelp.com
https://www.talkspace.com
https://www.pridecounseling.com
https://www.openpathcollective.org

ACKNOWLEDGMENTS

want to thank all the amazing contributors who shared their experiences with microaggressions. Your courage to use your own pain to make a better world will forever inspire me.

I also want to thank those who've supported me during the process of making this book: this book wouldn't be possible without you, and I wouldn't be possible without you.

ABOUT THE CONTRIBUTORS

CHRISTINE AHANOTU is a creative producer based in Los Angeles. Born to an Irish mother and a Nigerian father, she often marvels at the many ways identity manifests and affects us all.

AKEEM OMAR ALI is an artist, scholar, actor, consultant, and writer. As a seventh-generation American, Akeem comes from a big family of athletes, bus drivers, community organizers, educators, musicians, military service members, and grocers. Ali recently completed a master's degree in national security from King's College London and is the first masculine-presenting Black person to graduate from the Performance Studies BA program at NYU Tisch. Ali believes there's a direct connection between politics and the arts.

ANONYMOUS is an active community member within the Indigenous diaspora community based in Tongva Territory, dedicated to social and environmental justice.

AWAKOKO is an actor who was born in South Sudan and moved to the United States with her family at the age of eight. Before she took up acting, Awakoko was and still is a licensed nurse.

REBECCA BARNES is a Jewish girl born and raised in Los Angeles, California, currently residing in Ventura County. She is an entrepreneur and business owner with a background in fitness, sales, and business management. She is a dog and cat lover and a mom of three fur babies.

PRISCILLA BONNET is an Australian comedy writer based in Los Angeles. She most recently sold a half-hour comedy to ABC/Disney called *Dairy Kween*, based on the true-life story of the author of this book! She is married with two boys and currently undergoing IVF, where she is forcing her doctor to do whatever it takes to create a girl!

KEAH BROWN is an award-winning journalist and author of *The Pretty One*, *Sam's Super Seats*, and *The Secret Summer Promise*. Find out more about her at keahbrown.com.

RICHARDSON CHERY is a Haitian American actor, producer, and humanitarian and a graduate of the American Academy of Dramatic Arts in Los Angeles, California. Richardson was born and raised in Port-au-Prince, Haiti, and resides in Los Angeles, where he focuses on supporting the Haitian community through film, activities, and social awareness. Richardson has an insatiable passion for filmmaking and acting, and in accordance with this, he always brings his absolute best to every single project he works on.

Born and raised in Lima, Peru, ENRIQUE CHIABRA moved to the US when he was thirteen. He is a journalist and local news anchor in Los Angeles.

SUSAN COLE is an award-winning health activist, writer, broadcaster, and public speaker. She is a passionate advocate for global health equity and accessible information, particularly for people living with HIV, for whom she's been advocating for two decades.

MORGAN ELIZABETH is a mommy as well as a three-time NAACP award-winning producer and director who loves to put a smile on people's faces.

An old and creative soul, MITCHELL FAHEY loves to hang with his two cats, write in his journal daily, practice his spirituality and expression through dance, and take time for meditation and mindfulness walks every day. In 2018, he moved out to Los Angeles, California, to pursue his dreams of creating his vision of a happy and successful life on the West Coast. Mitchell tries to put the best version of himself out into the universe and strongly believes in wearing your heart on your sleeve and being open to love.

ALEXANDRA FOLSTER is a creative director and film photographer based out of Detroit and NYC.

JESSICA MARIE GARCIA is an actress, writer, producer. She is most recognizable for her work as Jasmine Flores on the hit Netflix show *On My Block*.

GIGI GORGEOUS GETTY is a YouTube star, transgender activist, author, television personality, actress, model, and LGBTQIA+ icon. Gigi is an advisor to the Ariadne Getty Foundation and works closely with several LGBTQ organizations including GLAAD, Los Angeles LGBT Center, the Trevor Project, and the Children's Hospital of LA Transyouth Program. Additionally, Gigi has been named in *TIME* magazine's "25 Most Influential People on the Internet" and *Forbes* "30 Under 30" lists. In May 2023, Gigi, alongside coauthor Gottmik, released their book *The T Guide*, a body of work dedicated to discussing the ins and outs of being transgender with honest and hilarious tales of what it means to be true to oneself.

NATS GETTY is an artist, activist, philanthropist, and designer with an enduring passion for self-expression and radical social progress. Nats began his art career in 2014 when he discovered the therapeutic benefits of adding an artistic practice to his hectic life as a punk-infused Getty living in the public eye. These days, Nats uses mixed media to convey his bold message of civil rights and anti-fascism in his large-formatat paintings and fashion label. He is a champion of LGBTQ+ rights and advancing the global fight against discrimination and prejudice.

CAROLINA GUTIERREZ is an actor from Barranquilla, Colombia, now living in Los Angeles, California. Carolina has appeared in TV shows Like *NCIS: Los Angeles*, *The L Word: Generation Q*, and *Scorpion*. As a proud Latina transgender woman, Carolina has advocated for her community through various platforms, and she hopes to continue to make an impact in the world through her art, philanthropy, and entrepreneurial endeavors.

JAZZMYNE JAY is a Midwestern-raised, corn-fed lesbian who lives in Los Angeles. She is a content creator, personality, and semi-decent twerker. Through honestly a dope fashion sense, mental health talks, and journeys about self-love and empowerment—Jazzmyne Jay will continue to hype you up and be your Libra Queen.

SANDER JENNINGS is a digital marketing leader and social influencer committed to effectuating positive change in the world. Through his consistent portrayal of allyship to his 1.1 million followers on social media and his active participation on the reality TV show *I Am Jazz*, Sander is a role model on how to spread unconditional love, support, and optimism to those around him.

CORNELIUS JONES JR. is a multidisciplinary performing artist and wellness coach who has performed on Broadway and in theatres across the US and internationally. In the wellness community, he's led numerous yoga teacher trainings, curated a plethora of hybrid yoga classes, and coaches yoga teachers on how to sustain their voice while teaching. Additionally, Cornelius is an Ayurvedic Wellness Counselor, is a self-published author, and works independently in the field of addiction and recovery as a creative arts and healing facilitator.

FREDERICK JOSEPH is the author of two instant *New York Times* bestsellers, *The Black Friend: On Being a Better White Person* and *Patriarchy Blues: Reflections on Manhood*, a collection of essays and poetry. He is also the author of the picture book *Black Panther: Wakanda Forever: The Courage to Dream*. An award-winning activist, philanthropist, and marketing professional, Frederick was named to the 2019 *Forbes* "30 Under 30" list, is a recipient of the Bob Clampett Humanitarian Award, and was selected for the 2018 Root 100, an annual list of the most influential African Americans.

STEPHANIE KWONG is the cofounder and CEO of the Rapid Rewire Method, a global training company teaching a suite of transformational tools that clears out any problems, stress, limiting beliefs, and even trauma in less than an hour, sometimes as quickly as fifteen minutes. Her work proves that shifting from a life of limitation and stress to one of power and freedom is possible, and with the Rapid Rewire Method, she's making that shift fast, painless, and sustainable.

Joel L. Daniels, also known as **JOÉL LEON**, is a Bronx-born and raised performer, father, author, and storyteller who writes and tells stories for Black people. He is the author of the 2024 essay collection *Everything and Nothing at Once.*

MELANIA LUISA MARTE is a writer, poet, and musician from New York living between the Dominican Republic and Texas. Marte's debut collection of poetry, *Plantains and Our Becoming*, was published by Tiny Reparations, an imprint of Plume and Penguin Random House, in 2023. You can follow her journey on social media: @MelaTocaTierra.

JESSE MEDINA is an eight-year active-duty veteran of the United States Army. He has experience in training, operations, and management within the armed forces, retail, and nonprofit sector. As a transgender man of color, Jesse has played a vital role in ensuring transgender men of color are included in all conversations by remaining openly visible within every space he navigates in and through.

ZACH MIKO was the first plus-sized male model signed to a major agency. He has starred in campaigns for Dolce and Gabbana, Gap, LL Bean, and more than fifty international brands. He was a guest judge on *America's Next Top Model* and has launched his own plus-sized swimwear line, Meekos. He is also an actor, a graduate of the American Academy of Dramatic Arts, and a writer, soon releasing his first memoir.

JOCELYN MONDRAGON-ROSAS, also known as Jocy at @ jocyofthedragons across all social media platforms, is a disabled Chicana activist, speaker, and influencer from southern Louisiana. She's dedicated to building community by sharing her disability and her Mexican roots through a political and creative lens online. Jocelyn has been featured on *NowThis*, ABC, *BuzzFeed*, and more.

JESSE MONTANA moved to Los Angeles to pursue a career in music and ended up becoming a celebrity stylist and reality TV personality. His work ethic, passion, and creativity have helped him to be successful in his various roles. He used social media to help launch his career. He wrote his first song off of his EP, "Drunk On You," which was produced by a Grammy award-winning producer, and his career took off from there. His position now as a fashion digital creator, artist, stylist, and musician helps keep his career exciting and diverse with big things on the horizon.

JENNIFER P. is an intuitive, creative, empire-building badass. She consults internationally and finds immense joy in helping others reach their highest potential . . . here or in the multiverse.

JEREMIAH RIPLEY (he/they) is a queer-intersex actor, writer, and educator. He was born and raised in the foothills of the Appalachian mountains. Jeremiah lives in Los Angeles with his partner, Griff, and their dog, Jack.

R.K. RUSSELL is a former NFL player, a social justice advocate, and the author of *The Yards Between Us*. In August of 2019, Russell made history by becoming the first out active NFL player to identify as bisexual. A decorated defensive end who has played for the Dallas Cowboys and the Tampa Bay Buccaneers, he has sacked Hall of Famers and gone up against the fiercest competitors at the height of their game.

PHIL SAMBA is a London-based writer, social activist, health promoter, and researcher working in public health. He's written for the BBC, the *Guardian*, *Huck Magazine*, and *Gay Times*.

PRITESH SHAH is an actor, comedian, writer, and producer. Pritesh has appeared in dozens of hit television shows, including *Grimm, Criminal Minds: Beyond Borders, Game of Silence*, recurring on the Emmy-nominated *Six* on the History Channel, and on the pilot of *The Walking Dead: The World Beyond*. In 2021, Pritesh released his short film *Invisible Brown Man*, which was cowritten with Black List writer Dennis Fallon. He released it on YouTube, and it quickly became a viral sensation on TikTok, reaching ten million views. He just had his directorial debut on his latest film, *Two Indians*, a Civil War Western drama.

SJ SINDU is an award-winning Tamil diaspora author of four books, including the most recent, *Shakti* and *The Goth House Experiment*. A Lambda Literary fellow, Sindu holds a PhD in creative writing and is an assistant professor at Virginia Commonwealth University.

BRIAN MICHAEL SMITH is an actor and advocate best known for breaking ground in trans masculine representation in television. After appearances on *Chicago P.D.* and *Homeland*, Smith ushered in a trifecta of trans male characters beginning with Toine Wilkins in OWN's *Queen Sugar*, followed by Pierce Williams in Showtime's *The L Word: Generation Q* and most notably as firefighter Paul Strickland in Fox's *9-1-1 Lone Star*, in which he became the first out Black trans man cast in a series regular role on network TV. Smith continues to use his visibility and platforms to advocate for better representation of trans people in TV and film and equality for all.

FRAN TIRADO is a writer, editor, and filmmaker who most recently ran LGBTQ+ audience strategy at Netflix. She works in Brooklyn and LA. @fransquishco.

JACOB TOBIA (they/them) is a writer, producer, actor, and respectable nonbinary lady who doesn't yell at cops, believes that capitalism is super, and began identifying as nonbinary a full decade before it was cool. Their debut memoir *Sissy: A Coming-of-Gender Story* was a national bestseller, a testament to both their striking prose and ability to convince people to purchase things. Their work has been featured in the *New York Times*, the *Washington Post*, *Cosmopolitan*, and too many other places to list without being annoying. A proud member of the Arab American community, they pass as white and can't speak Arabic, so no one cares.

RAIN VALDEZ is an actress, writer, producer, and out-and-proud Filipino transgender woman most notably of the 2022 GLAAD Listed for *Re-Live*, *Ryans, Hexed*, and the series *Razor Tongue*. Rain's unique writing and performance on *Razor Tongue* earned her a Primetime Emmy nomination for "Outstanding Actress in a Short Form Comedy or Drama Series" and a "Special Recognition" GLAAD Award. Her writing and performance in the rom-com short film *Ryans* earned her a Best North American Short Film Award at OUTSouth Queer Film Festival, and *Hexed* earned her three nominations for Best Director, Best Actress, and Best Short at the Madrid International Film Festival. She is the Trailblazer Award recipient at the 2021 Outfest Legacy Awards.

ELISABET VELASQUEZ is an award-winning Boricua writer. Her debut young adult novel in verse, *When We Make It*, went on to receive wide recognition, including being named as a *New York Times* Young Adult Book to Watch For. When she is not writing, she is living the life she hopes to write about.

JANE VELEZ-MITCHELL is an award-winning TV journalist, *New York Times* bestselling author, documentary filmmaker, and the founder and president of UnchainedTV, a free, global, streaming TV network to promote a compassionate, sustainable, plant-based lifestyle, part of UnchainedTV.com, her California-based nonprofitrofit. She lives with her dog and cat in Los Angeles.

MARQUISE VILSÓN is an actor and activist of the trans masculine experience. Marquise has been seen on TV in *Tom Swift* (series regular), *A League of Their Own, Quantum Leap, Law & Order: SVU* (GLAAD award nominee), *Bull, The Blacklist, Tales of The City,* and *Blindspot*, and the films *The Kitchen, Ben Is Back*, and *B-Boy Blues*. He shares his experiences of Black Trans masculine visibility in documentaries *Pride* and *Disclosure*, and he was also featured in the documentary film *No Ordinary Man*. A long-standing member and participant of the underground ballroom scene, Marquise is a force and well-respected leader in the ballroom community, having walked numerous categories over the last two-plus decades. Acknowledged by his ballroom family and nonprofit sectors alike for his visibility and community work, Marquise has been presented with the Eric Christian Bazaar Award, Octavia St. Laurent Trans Activist Award, the Masquerade Blue Print Award, and deemed a Transman ICON and was inducted into the Dorian Corey Hall of Fame for all his contributions.

KAWASI WESTON is an award-winning singer, songwriter, and vocal producer. After graduating from Morehouse College and attending Princeton University, he shifted his career from foreign affairs to more domestic, using law and music as his anchors.

CEDRICK WILEY is an artist, writer, philosopher, and veteran. He is a marine veteran with a passion for the way life works.

OMKARI L. WILLIAMS is a speaker, host of the podcast *Stepping into Truth*, and author of the book *Micro Activism: How You Can Make a Difference in the World (Without a Bullhorn)*. She is focused on spreading the philosophy of how small, sustainable actions can make a big impact.

KO WILLS is an actress, activist, plus-size model, and professional makeup artist working in Los Angeles.

MARS ELLIOT WRIGHT is a trans artist, fashion designer, and activist. He's a mixed-media artist who is interested in the beauty of imperfection and the strength of radical honesty. Through sharing his life vulnerably, he hopes to help folks feel less alone.

ZACHARY ZANE is the author of *Boyslut: A Memoir and Manifesto*. He writes "Sexplain It," the sex and relationship advice column at *Men's Health*, and "Navigating Non-Monogamy," the polyamorous relationship column at *Cosmo*. His work has been featured in *New York Times, Rolling Stone, Washington Post, Playboy*, and more.

ABOUT THE AUTHORS

BILLIE LEE is a writer, actress, producer, and stand-up comedian who has performed across the country. She was the first openly transgender cast member on Bravo's *Vanderpump Rules* and has continued to be an outspoken voice for the LGBTQIA+ community. Billie is also an avid animal rights activist, which inspired the creation of She's So Vegan, a lifestyle brand that promotes kindness to ourselves, our animals, and the planet. She is currently living and working in Los Angeles and recording her first podcast, *Billie and the Kid*, produced by comedy powerhouse Jam In The Van.

DR. GINA C. TORINO received her PhD in counseling psychology from Columbia University and is currently an interim dean for the School of Social and Behavioral Sciences at SUNY's Empire State University. She has published widely on topics such as cultural competency development, microaggressions, White racial identity development, and teaching strategies that promote cultural self-awareness. Dr. Torino and her team provide specialized diversity consultation services to corporate and nonprofit organizations. Her recent publications include *Microaggression Theory: Influence and Implications* as well as many influential articles on the topic of microaggressions.